My Grandmother's Kitchen

Books by Madame Benoit

Madame Benoit's World of Food
Madame Benoit's Microwave Cook Book
Madame Benoit Cooks at Home
Madame Benoit's Lamb Cookbook
Encyclopedia of Canadian Cooking
Canadiana Cookbook
My Secrets for Better Cooking
The Best of Jehane Benoit

My Grandmother's Kitchen

Jehane Benoit

McGraw-Hill Ryerson Limited

Toronto Montreal New York St. Louis
San Francisco Auckland Bogotá Guatemala
Hamburg Johannesburg Lisbon London Madrid
Mexico New Delhi Panama Paris San Juan
São Paulo Singapore Sydney Toyko

1 2 3 4 5 6 7 8 9 10D 0 9 8 7 6 5 4 3 2 1

Printed and bound in Canada

ISBN 0-07-548043-3

This book was originally published in French under the
title Secrets et Recettes du Cahier de ma Grand-mère.

Canadian Cataloguing in Publication Data

Benoit, Jehane, date
MY GRANDMOTHER'S KITCHEN
Revision of French version published by Editions Beau-
chemin, Montreal, 1959, with title: Secrets et recettes du
cahier de ma grand'mère.
Includes index.
ISBN 0-07-548043-3

1. Cookery, French-Canadian. I. Title.

TX715.B4513   641.59714   C81-094495-2

From the notebook of
My Grandmother,
Rosana Beaudin Cardinal,
A collection of many favorite recipes
Written in the eighteenth-century manner
and
Passed on to my mother Louise
and
Adapted for the twentieth century by me
and
Passed on to my daughter Monique
who
Passes it on to her children.

I dedicate this book to
Marie Syrkin, the poet, who wrote:

"I carry my seventy years
Like a woman with child.
They are in me, fateful and foolish
Absolute, wild.
They cannot be born into time
To sicken or bloom;
Then why do they grapple and stir
As though in a womb?"

Contents

Introduction

Food is so much a part of the many happy childhood hours I spent at my grandparents' home that writing this little book was, I felt, a tribute to my mother's mother. To her, cooking was an art, and as in all arts, as she often said, simplicity breeds perfection. There may have been only bread and butter on the table, but the bread was homemade with freshly ground wheat, beautifully shaped and crusty, the butter creamy and freshly churned.

My grandmother was *petite*, full of life, and, needless, to say, *gourmande*. When asked for one of her recipes, she would answer, like so many of the women of her time, "Put a little of this, a little of that, let your nose and your heart do the adding, and cook until done!"

This is how much of our Canadian cuisine came about. Our mothers used their noses and their hearts in cooking. They had to be inventive since, unlike today, so many ingredients were not readily available. Most food had to be grown at home and kept in root cellars during the winter, or buried in the snow to freeze. Cookbooks were rare, and cooking schools didn't exist. Nowadays, with the great rush and efficiency in our lives, we seem to have lost our feeling for and insight into cuisine.

My grandmother taught me, a long time ago, that our cooking is part of our folklore, and it must therefore be varied. It bears testimony to our past, to our mothers' ingenuity, and to the spirit of our own flesh and blood.

She used to say to me, "Come, I'll tell you about our cuisine" . . . and she would talk about the old customs, the ways of preparing a dish, and the legend behind it —

1

describing it all in such a wonderful language! Even though I was young, I was fully aware of what she was saying, and I understood her clearly.

One day, in a little old straw basket, I uncovered her precious recipes written in her little book of "secrets," tattered and torn by the years, full of tricks of the trade and advice based on her personal experience. I thought to myself, "Now is the time for me to reveal my grandmother's cuisine," which is also that of your grandmothers. So, let's close our eyes and listen to the soup kettle boiling ever so gently, smell the simmering stew, the broiling chops, and the fragrance of gingerbread permeating the air. Hand in hand, let's all get together and round up our innumerable old recipes.

I shall not give you the recipes exactly as I found them written in my grandmother's old notebook, because they were written in an old-fashioned culinary language, difficult to understand at times. To prove my point, here is a sample of what I read.

Salt Pork Pancake

3 bowlfuls of flour, diluted in enough fresh milk for a slightly thick pancake batter. Add eggs — more or less — according to the day.

Fry slices of petit salé *in lard . . .*

As you can see, the language is not perfectly clear. I had to test many of the recipes first, and then give them a modern touch. Except where otherwise indicated, each recipe will serve about four people. I cannot begin to tell you what pleasure I derived from revising these old recipes, many of which have almost ceased to exist. I sincerely hope that they will also bring you many happy hours in the kitchen and at the table.

I have included all the comments and names that appeared in the recipes. These remarks gave me the feeling that they would create a bond between you and me, to make us feel like one big family in my grandmother's kitchen.

So come cook and eat, one and all!

Beverages and Soups

Rosana's Dandelion Wine
Vin de pissenlit de Rosana

An excellent, very old recipe, which will also encourage you to clear your lawn of early spring dandelions. Beware — it is very potent once it has fermented.

Gather young dandelion blooms in the early morning, preferably after a heavy rain. Cut off the stems, because they would make the wine bitter.

Place **2 quarts (2 L) dandelion blooms** in a crock. Pour **2 quarts (2 L) boiling water** on top, add **2 lemons** and **2 oranges,** unpeeled and thinly sliced. Let the crock stand 2 days, uncovered, in a cool place. A cold pantry is better than the refrigerator.

Once the steeping period is over, pour the liquid through a sieve, crushing the blooms as much as possible. Bring the liquid to boil. In the meantime, place **1 lb. (500 g) sugar** in a pie plate and heat it in a 300°F. (150°C) oven. Pour the hot sugar into the boiling liquid. Bring the mixture back to boil, and let it boil for 2 minutes. Return this syrup to the crock, filling it only ⅔ because the fermentation process could cause the liquid to overflow.

Sprinkle **1 envelope active dry yeast** in the juice of ½ **orange,** let stand 5 minutes, stir, and add to the syrup. Mix well, return to the cold room, and let it ferment for 3 to 5 days without moving the crock or stirring the syrup. A cheesecloth may be placed over the top to prevent dust from falling in.

Sterilize the bottle and pour in the fermented juice through a filter, filling only to ¾. You many buy filter paper at a drugstore, or use milk filters, sold at special stores for dairy farmers. Cork and keep 3 to 4 months in a cool room. The wine becomes stronger as it matures, and in time it becomes golden clear.

Haytime Lemonade
Limonade des foins

Grand-mère's lemonade is the very best. To spike it (she never did), add 1 cup (250 mL) dry gin or vodka or white rum. Enjoy!

Cut **4 peeled lemons** into thin slices and remove seeds. Add **¾ cup (180 mL) sugar.** Let stand 10 to 15 minutes, then press firmly with potato masher to extract all the juice and oil from the sliced lemons.

Add **4–5 cups (1–1¼ L) well water** (or very cold water from the tap) and continue pressing fruit until water is flavored. Add ice (use **1 tray of ice cubes**). When it is chilled, taste for sweetness, adding more sugar if you so wish.

Raspberry Shrub
Sirop de vinaigre aux framboises

All my life, this has been my favorite beverage. My grand-mother made it perfectly.

Refrigerate it once the bottle has been opened. It will keep 2 to 3 years. It's super served as syrup over custards, pancakes, or apple desserts, or in gin and soda with ice.

Place in an earthenware crock **3 quarts (3 L) cider vinegar** and **10 lb. (5 kg) fresh raspberries**, preferably picked early in the morning. Let stand 4 days in a warm place.

Pour the juice through a sieve, pressing on fruit to extract all the juice, and measure. Bring to boil. Add to boiling juice **1 lb. (500 g) sugar** for each quart (1 L) of juice and cook, while stirring, just enough to melt the sugar. Bottle. Serve with well water (if you have a well) or soda.

Grand-mère's Mulled Apple Cider
La bolée de jus de pommes épicé

This was an autumn treat, shared when the neighbors came to help gather the ripe apples. When the work was done, they had this mulled cider with big baskets of doughnuts. Then they all danced to the accompaniment of the violin.

Boil together **1½ cups (375 mL) sugar** and **4 cups (1 L) water** for 5 minutes. Remove from heat and add **2 cinnamon sticks, 8 whole allspice berries, 10 peppercorns, 1 piece fresh *or* dry ginger,** cut in 3. Cover and let stand 12 hours on the kitchen counter.

To serve, bring to boil **3 quarts (3 L) apple juice *or* cider** and **2 cups (500 mL) fresh lemon juice,** then add the spiced syrup. Strain and serve immediately.

Dry Bread Soup
Panade de pain sec

This is a bread soup based on a recipe from the Poitou region of France. Grand-mère's friend from Bretagne gave it to her, and I am still enjoying it!

I put in a saucepan 2–3 **cups (250–375 mL) dried bread,** *cut into small pieces, over which I pour* 8 **cups (2 L) tepid water,** *and let stand half an hour. In the meantime, I fry* 2–3 **onions** *in my* **chicken fat** *and add a little* **savory.** *Then I add the onions to the bread and bring the whole to a slow boil, stirring vigorously. I cover the pan and let the soup simmer very gently for 20 minutes.*

To serve, I **salt** *to taste and add* 1 **egg** *beaten slightly with* ½ **cup (125 mL) milk** *and a good piece of* **butter.** *I stir and serve.*

Christmas Oyster Soup
Soupe aux huitres de Noël

This traditional Québec dish is still very much alive. My grandmother's recipe is, as far as I am concerned, the best there is.

Peel and grate in long, thin shreds **2 medium carrots** and add ½ **cup (125 mL) finely diced celery.** Melt ¼ **cup (60 mL) unsalted butter** in a saucepan, and add the vegetables. Stir. Cover and simmer over very low heat for 20 minutes, without browning the vegetables.

Add **4 cups (1 L) milk** (or use half milk, half cream). Bring to boil.

Heat **4 cups (1 L) oysters** in an enamelled cast-iron pan over medium heat; do not boil. Pour into the milk and serve. The soup should be served as soon as ready, otherwise it tends to curdle. The milk and vegetables can be prepared ahead of time, and the oysters heated and added at the last moment. **Salt and pepper** to taste.

Breads

Cabbage Leaf Bread
Pain à la feuille de chou

I never fail to make this bread whenever I serve game birds. Grand-mère used whole wheat bread, but any type will do. The cabbage leaves can also be tied around the bread with coarse thread, for an even more pronounced flavor.

*When I have some **risen bread dough**, I shape some into 2 round loaves, I cover the top of each one with **a large cabbage leaf**, and place it on **another cabbage leaf**. Then I let the dough rise in a warm place until double in bulk.*

The loaves are placed in the oven with the cabbage leaves. When cooked, the leaves are removed, leaving an interesting imprint on the bread and giving it a delicious flavor.

Easter Sunday Holy Bread
Le pain bénit de monsieur le Curé

Like many other women in the parish, Grand-mère made this bread on Easter Saturday and gave it to Monsieur le Curé for Easter Sunday mass. The breads were diced, blessed, and passed to the congregation on a silver tray.

Dissolve **2 tsp. (10 mL) sugar** in **1 cup (250 mL) warm water.** Add **2 envelopes active dry yeast,** let stand 10 minutes, then stir well.

Blend together in a large bowl **1 cup (250 mL) scalded milk, ½ cup (125 mL) butter, 2 tsp. (10 mL) salt, ½ cup (125 mL) sugar.** Mix well and cool.

Beat **4 eggs** until light and lemon colored.

Add the well-stirred yeast to the cooled mixture. Stir, add the beaten eggs and **½ tsp. (2 mL) almond extract.** Fold in **6–7 cups (1.5–1.75 L) sifted all-purpose flour,** and when the dough is firm enough to knead, turn onto a floured board and knead lightly 3 to 4 minutes. Dough should be soft but not sticky. An extra ¼ cup (60 mL) flour may be used for kneading. Place the dough in a greased bowl. Cover with a clean cloth and let rise in a warm place, free from draught, for about 2 hours or until double in bulk.

Punch down the dough and bring the sides to the middle. Turn onto a floured board and knead into a ball. Divide in 2 equal parts. Sprinkle each with **½ tsp. (2 mL) aniseed,** then knead into a ball. Cover with a clean cloth and let stand 10 minutes.

Shape the balls so that they will fit easily in 2 greased pans. Brush tops with melted butter. Cover with a clean cloth and let rise in a warm place, free from draught, about 1 hour or until double in bulk. Bake 40 to 50 minutes in a 375°F. (190°C) oven. Unmold and cool on a cake rack.

"Cretons" Bread
Le pain aux cretons

For a variation, my grandmother often "sowed" raisins, as she used to say, on top of the dough. I am not aware of any recipe for this wonderful bread that exists outside my family. My grandmother said she learned it from her mother-in-law. Should anyone else have this recipe, I would be happy to hear from that person.

Cut ¼ **lb. (125 g) salt pork** (it should be rather fat) into very small pieces. Brown over medium heat until completely melted. Drain and cool the fat.

Use half the recipe for risen dough for Scottish Oatmeal Bread (see page 9). Knead and roll ½ inch (1.25 cm) thick.

Spread the melted pork fat generously on the dough. Sprinkle all over with **dark brown sugar** and **cloves** and **cinnamon** to taste. Dot with the tiny golden bits of pork fat, strained from the fat.

Roll like a jelly roll. Place in a greased loaf pan and let rise until double in bulk. Bake 1 hour in a 375°F. (190°C) oven. Unmold immediately. Slice and eat as you would raisin bread.

Scottish Oatmeal Bread
Pain de l'Ecossais à la soupane

Oatmeal was always referred to, whether dry or cooked, as *soupane,* or *grains écossais,* because all the Scots ate oatmeal and taught the Québec women how to use it. So, for the Québec people, oatmeal bread could be nothing but Scottish.

Dissolve **1 tsp. (5 mL) sugar** in ½ **cup (125 mL) hot water** then add **1 envelope active dry yeast.** Let stand 10 minutes.

Pour **2 cups (500 mL) boiling water** over **2 cups (500 mL) oatmeal.** Add **2 tbsp. (500 mL) bacon fat** or other fat of your choice and ½ **cup (125 mL) molasses.** Mix. Cool until tepid; add the yeast.

Add **2 cups (500 mL) whole wheat flour** and **2 tbsp. (30 mL) wheat germ.** Mix thoroughly and let rise in a warm place until the dough is very light, about 1 hour.

Add approximately **2 cups (500 mL) all-purpose flour** and **1 tbsp. (15 mL) salt.** Knead dough and place in a bowl. Cover with a cloth and let rise in a warm place until double in bulk, about 2 hours. Punch down. Knead for a few moments. Divide in 2. Shape into 2 loaves and place in oiled bread pans. Let rise once again until double in bulk. Bake 1 hour in a 375 °F. (190 °C) oven. Unmold immediately and cool on a cake rack.

Potato Water Bread
Le pain à l'eau de patates

In winter, our pioneers often ate for breakfast cold salt pork, very thinly sliced, with boiled potatoes. After breakfast homemade bread was prepared for the next day, using the potato cooking water. My grandmother always added 2 or 3 mashed potatoes to her bread dough. It was super!

Heat until slightly more than tepid **1 cup (250 mL) potato cooking water,** melt in it **1 tsp. (5 mL) sugar** and sprinkle top with **1 envelope active dry yeast.** Let stand 10 minutes.

Place in a large bowl **3 cups (750 mL) hot potato water;** add **3 tbsp. (50 mL) sugar, 5 tsp. (25 mL) salt, 2 mashed potatoes,** the well-stirred yeast, **6 cups (1.5 L) all-purpose flour.** Beat together to blend thoroughly. Add **1 tbsp. (15 mL) shortening, 2 tbsp. (30 mL) soft butter,** an additional **4 cups (1 L) flour.** Mix and knead 10 minutes.

Return dough to a bowl and let stand in a warm place until double in bulk. Then punch down dough and let rise a second time until double in bulk. Each time, it will take approximately 70 to 80 minutes for the dough to rise.

Punch down dough and divide in 3 to 4 parts. Let stand 10 minutes on the pastry board, covered with a cloth.

Knead and shape each piece of dough into a round ball. Place on a greased cookie sheet. Let rise once again until double in bulk, about 45 minutes. Bake in a 400 °F. (200 °C) oven 35 to 40 minutes or until golden brown. Cool on a cake rack.

Pancakes and Porridge

Apple Pancakes from the Townships
Crêpes aux pommes des Cantons

Each year at the end of September, the whole family would go to the Eastern Townships Apple Festival. And there, instead of eggs in syrup, as was the custom at sugaring parties, apple pancakes were served with lots of butter and delicious Townships maple syrup. Little did I know that one day we would have a farm near the place where the Festival was held.

Sift together **2 cups (500 mL) all-purpose flour, 1 tbsp. (15 mL) baking powder** (no error), **1 tsp. (5 mL) soda, 2 tsp. (10 mL) salt, 3 tbsp. (50 mL) sugar, 1 tsp. (5 mL) cinnamon.**

Beat **2¼ cups (560 mL) sour milk** and **2 eggs** in a bowl. Add **1 cup (250 mL) apples,** unpeeled and cut in small pieces, and **6 tbsp. (90 mL) melted butter.**

Add the sour milk mixture to the dry ingredients. Stir well. Cook as you would ordinary pancakes, in a lightly greased cast-iron frying pan. Brown on both sides. Serve plain or with butter or syrup.

Breadcrumb Pancakes
Crêpes à la mie de pain

What a way to use dry bread! I have made these often through the years and anyone who tastes them is intrigued. They look and taste like pancakes, yet have a subtle difference no one can describe.

Pour **1½ cups (325 mL) hot milk** over **1½ cups (325 mL) dried bread,** broken into small pieces. Add **a good-sized piece of butter** and let stand 15 minutes. Then, add **2 beaten eggs, ½ cup (125 mL) flour, 3 tsp.(15 mL) baking powder, salt, 1 tbsp. (15mL) sugar.** Mix together and cook as you would pancakes, on a greased griddle.

Serve with butter and syrup or with creamed salmon or scrambled eggs.

St. Rémi Buckwheat Pancakes
Galettes de sarrazin de St-Rémi

My grandmother, who was a "Beaudin from St. Rémi," used to say, "We, the Beaudins, make the best pancakes in the whole townships." I must admit they were fantastic, and nowadays I still use her recipe as I have never encountered another that surpasses it.

Stir to melt **1 tsp. (5 mL) sugar** in **½ cup (125 mL) warm water.** Add **1 envelope active dry yeast.** Let stand 10 minutes. Stir, then add **2 cups (500 mL) tepid water, ½ cup (125 mL) sugar, 1½ tsp. (7 mL) salt.**

Fold in **1 cup (250 mL) all-purpose flour** and **2 cups (500 mL) buckwheat flour.** Beat into a smooth cream. Cover and refrigerate overnight.

In the morning, add **1 tsp. (5 mL) soda** and ½ cup (125 mL) cream. Mix together. Let stand 30 minutes at room temperature. Cook them like ordinary pancakes. Serve with whipped butter or maple syrup.

Hominy Corn Pancakes
Les crêpes au blé d'inde lessivé

Blé d'inde lessivé or hominy corn is bought in cans, sometimes as lye corn. The Indians, who taught our ancestors how to make lye corn, refer to it as *sacamité* and still use it today. Hominy pancakes are still very popular in Vermont, USA.

On the first Friday of each month, Grandmother always served hominy pancakes for breakfast, after mass. This was also my mother's custom, and I, too, have kept it alive. We eat them with molasses or maple syrup and butter.

First, mash to a pulp **2 cups (500 mL) cooked hominy corn** with a wooden pestle. Add **1 tsp. (5 mL) salt, 2 tsp. (10 mL) baking powder, 1 cup (250 mL) flour.** When everything is well blended, add **3 cups (750 mL) fresh** *or* **sour milk** and **3 beaten eggs.** Then cook them as you would ordinary pancakes.

Indian Pancakes
Crêpes des sauvages

The Indians made these pancakes with cornmeal and cooked them on flat heated stones. This recipe is lighter, using white flour. I have occasionally served these pancakes at barbecues, cooking them on stones heated over charcoal. My guests are always delighted.

Mix together **1 tbsp. (15 mL) sugar, 1 tsp. (5 mL) baking soda, 1 cup (250 mL) sour cream, ¾ cup (180 mL) milk** *or* **water.** Add enough **flour [about 2 cups (500 mL)]** to make a light pancake batter. Pour into a large milk jug and cover with a cloth. Leave overnight on the kitchen table. In the morning, the dough will have fermented.

Add **1 tsp. (5 mL) salt.** Stir well and drop by tablespoonfuls (15 mL) in a cast-iron frying pan, greased with **pork rind** *or* **bacon fat.** Serve with molasses or butter.

Salt Pork Pancakes
Crêpe "au lard d'habitant"

Salt pork is not always available, but thickly sliced bacon can replace it. Close to our farm there is an excellent country butcher who still makes *lard d'habitant,* as it was called. It is prepared from the same cut that is used to smoke bacon. In the old days, salt pork was neither smoked not salted, and it was thickly sliced.

So, during the past few years I have been able to make this crêpe following the authentic recipe left to us by my great-grandmother. Served with a green salad, it makes a perfect light meal.

Cut **4 slices fresh** *or* **salt pork** in 2-inch (5 cm) squares. Melt the squares in a cast-iron frying pan until well browned and crisp. Add **1 small onion,** thinly sliced. As soon as the lard has browned, pour the following pancake batter on top (do not remove any fat).

Mix together **1½ cups (375 mL) sour milk,** ½ **tsp. (2 mL) baking soda,** ½ **tsp. (2 mL) salt, 2 eggs,** enough **flour [about ¾ cup (180 mL)]** for a clear batter. Cook the pancake over low heat until the edges and bottom brown, then cover and cook over low heat another 15 minutes, or until well cooked. Sprinkle with minced parsley. To serve, cut in wedges.

Eulalie's Salt Pork Crêpe
Crêpe au lard d'Eulalie

Eulalie was one of my grandmother's sisters — merry, petite, and always laughing and singing. A very good singer and pianist, she would sing at high mass on Sundays and stir everyone's emotions. She always felt desperate about me because, as she used to say, I couldn't sing even two notes in tune. That has not changed.

The *crêpe au lard,* a traditional dish of old Québec, was Eulalie's super-star specialty. She cooked it to perfection. I make it often, especially in the winter. It makes an interesting lunch, served with broiled tomatoes or creamed cabbage with dill or green onions. Bacon can replace the thinly sliced salt pork — somewhat difficult to find at times — although the flavor is not quite the same.

Place in an iron frying pan (I recommend enamelled cast iron) **8–10 slices good lean and fat salt pork** (more fat than lean). Cover with cold water. Bring to boil over medium heat, then simmer for 2 minutes. Drain.

Return the frying pan to medium heat and cook the salt pork slices until browned on both sides and the fat is melted. Do not remove fat.

To prepare the pancake, break **4 eggs** in a bowl, add **5 tbsp. (75 mL) all-purpose flour**, **½ tsp. (2 mL) salt**, **¼ tsp. (1 mL) pepper**. Mix together, preferably with a rotary beater, to obtain a smooth dough.

Add **2 cups (500 mL) milk.** Mix well and pour over the browned salt pork and fat. Cook for 10 minutes without stirring. Lift the sides of the pancake, tilting the pan so that the uncooked portion will run under. After a few moments lower the heat as much as possible. Cover and cook 5 minutes. The crêpe can be very easily removed from the pan.

Honey Sauce for Pancakes
Sauce au miel pour les crêpes

Grandmother wrote:

My husband has suggested that I find a way of using our honey, as our production has been very good this year.[Delightful how women listened to men in those days!] *I believe the bees have greatly enjoyed the borage which I sowed around the hives. I made a sauce with a "thought to economy," and it is very good.*

I keep in the winter kitchen a large preserve jar ¾ filled with honey. When I peel oranges, I put little pieces of rind, with no white skin, in the honey — very little at a time. And I keep on adding to this until the jar is full. I stir each time; honey crystallizes fast.

To make my pancake sauce, I heat **½ cup (125 mL) orange honey** *with* **½ cup (60 mL) cream** *and* **1 tsp (5 mL) butter,** *or I cream together butter and honey, which melt on the hot pancakes.*

I also make wild rose honey the same way. In early spring, I gather some wild roses when they start to bloom, cut out the bits of white in the bottom, and beat them into the honey — as many as my fancy dictates. It is superb served with hot toasted English muffins. This honey will keep many months, like any other honey.

Buckwheat Porridge
La soupane au sarrazin

To crack whole buckwheat Grandmother would roll it in a linen cloth and crush it with a rolling pin or beat it with a wooden pestle. Nowadays you can buy ground buckwheat, often sold under the name of *kasha.*

Buckwheat is also excellent served as a vegetable. It is cooked in the same manner, but the brown sugar is omitted and a piece of butter is added just before serving.

Place in the top of a double boiler **1 cup (250 mL) cracked buckwheat** *(kasha),* **1 tsp. (5 mL) salt, 1 tbsp. (15 mL) brown sugar, 3 cups (750 mL) water.** Mix well. Cover and cook 20 to 25 minutes, making sure that the water boils constantly.

Prepare it in the evening. When cooked, shut off the heat and let stand overnight. It takes only 10 to 12 minutes to reheat your cereal.

Meats

Harvest Beef Roll
Roulade de boeuf de la moisson

At harvest time, there were always many mouths to feed. At noon, vegetable soup was served, followed by this thinly sliced beef roll and a huge potato salad. Grandmother often cooked the roll in the soup kettle the previous day, which made it even tastier. I also cook it in vegetable soup.

Ask your butcher for a thin, whole round steak. Remove fat and bones.

Prepare a dry bread stuffing with **1 cup (250 mL) dried bread,** broken up in small pieces, **2 large onions,** minced and fried in **melted beef fat, 3 grated carrots,** ½ **cup (125 mL) melted butter, 1 tsp. (5 mL) coarse salt,** ½ **tsp. (2 mL) celery seed,** ¼ **tsp. (1 mL) pepper,** ½ **tsp. (2 mL) dry mustard, a pinch of ground cloves, 1 tsp. (5 mL) cinnamon,** ½ **tsp. (2 mL) allspice.** Mix thoroughly and spread over the meat. Place meat on a clean square of cotton. Make a large tight roll and sew it up with heavy thread.

Place the roll in a kettle of boiling water (just enough water to cover the meat). Cover and simmer 4 hours; do not boil. After 2 hours of cooking, add **1 tbsp. (15 mL) coarse salt.** When cooked (Grandmother checked for doneness with a knitting needle), remove roll from water.

Set on a plate and cover with a board. Place a weight on top. When completely cooled, place in refrigerator. To serve, unwrap and slice thinly.

Nana's Lamb Stew
Le ragoût d'agneau de Nana (du rang d'en haut)

Nana was the wife of the village baker. The strange fact was that she *never* ate bread, but lots, and I do mean a lot, of potatoes. She said that anise and thyme enhanced the flavor of this economical stew.

Cut **1½ lb. (680 g) lamb shoulder** into 2-inch (5 cm) pieces (the trimmings from a leg of lamb, before roasting, can also be used). Mix together in a large plate **2 tbsp. (30 mL) flour,** ½ **tsp. (2 mL) salt,** ½ **tsp. (2 mL) thyme,** ¼ **tsp. (1 mL) savory.** Roll the meat in this mixture.

Brown meat in **3 tbsp. (50 mL) melted lamb fat** or other fat of your choice. Add **3 cups (750 mL) water** and ¼ **tsp. (1 mL) anise.** Bring to boil. Cover and cook over low heat until the meat is tender, about 1 hour.

Add **8 small onions,** whole, **3 carrots,** cut in thick slices, **2 peeled potatoes,** diced. Cover and simmer 20 to 25 minutes.

Mix 1 tbsp. (15 mL) of the remaining flour with ½ **cup (125 mL) cream.** Add to the cooked stew. Stir to make a smooth, creamy gravy.

"Gogue" of Lamb or Veal Blood
Utilisation du sang de veau ou de mouton

Lamb or veal blood is found in large Italian and Greek markets, sold in blocks, usually by the pound.

It is also a specialty of Normandy, where it is known as *gogue.*During the celebration of the tercentenary of Montreal, I owned a restaurant on St. Hélène's Island at the time. At dinner, we celebrated the "good table" of Normandie, Bretagne, and Poitou, the birthplaces of most of our French ancestors. My own background being Normandie, I especially enjoyed serving *les gogues,* which were in great demand. When asked what they were I said, "Eat them, and I shall be back with the recipe." No one could believe what they were made with; they found them so delicious!

Fry, **1–2 cups (250–500 mL)** chopped onion or an equal amount of green onions, in melted fat. Add **2–3 cups (500–750 mL) lamb blood** and **a dash of savory.** Mix well together, cover, and simmer 10 or 20 minutes. Very good served with mashed potatoes.

Gogue can also be prepared by frying **1 cup (250 mL) small pieces of salt pork,** and adding **garlic** and **parsley** to taste. Mix together with the lamb blood (for Sunday best, add a few spoonfuls of red wine), cover, and simmer 15 to 20 minutes. Grand-mère served this on large slices of homemade bread toasted on top of the stove, with a green bean salad.

Séraphin's Pork Shoulder Stuffed with Apples
L'épaule de porc farcie aux pommes de Séraphin

Séraphin's stuffed shoulder of pork or veal was a family favorite. Séraphin was an old lumberjack cook in the area where my grandparents lived, and he always made this dish for them as a Christmas gift. His recipe read: "You stuff the shoulder, you roast the meat in the wood stove, using only maple wood, well aged — otherwise it is not as good!"

Stuffing:
Melt ¼ **lb. (110 g) diced fat salt pork,** until crisp and brown. Remove the small pieces of browned meat from the frying pan with a perforated spoon. Add to the fat **½ cup (125 mL) chopped celery, 1 large onion,** chopped, ¼ **cup (60 mL) parsley.** Fry this savory mixture for 5 minutes over medium heat, stirring often. Remove from pan and add the small pieces of reserved browned meat.

Then place **5 diced unpeeled apples** in the frying pan and sprinkle with ⅓ **cup (80 mL) maple** *or* **brown sugar.** Cover and cook over very low heat until the apples are tender, approximately 5 to 8 minutes. Remove the lid and cook until the apple juice has evaporated. Pour the apples over the vegetables and add **2 cups (500 mL) breadcrumbs. Salt** and **pepper** to taste.

To Prepare Meat:
Ask the butcher to remove the bones from a **veal** *or* **pork shoulder.** Keep the bones; you will need them.

Spread the pork or veal shoulder on a board and rub the inside with ½ **lemon** (Séraphin used homemade vinegar). Sprinkle with about **1 tsp. (2 mL) savory,** and place the apple and bread stuffing in the middle. Then roll the shoulder like a jelly roll. Tie securely at different intervals to shape nicely.

Place the meat in a roasting pan and surround with the reserved bones. Pour **1 cup (250 mL) apple juice** on the meat. Cook in a 350°F. (180°C) oven 40 minutes per pound (500 g), without covering or basting. Serve hot or cold.

To serve cold, cool the meat and cover. It will keep 4 to 5 days, refrigerated. Leave at room temperature for about 1 hour before serving.

Odilon's Jellied Pork
La galantine de porc du gros Odilon

Odilon was my grandfather's brother-in-law. He seemed to live for eating, which was foremost in his mind at all times. Because of his size, he was called *"le gros* Odilon."

He was always in such a happy mood when discussing recipes, and always our own, as he was devoted to Québec cuisine. This jellied pork dates far back in our culinary history, and when well prepared, it is a masterpiece. The bottom layer consists of a well-flavored brown jelly, covered by a layer of meat broken up into long slivers and surrounded with the fat. To be in keeping with tradition, this dish should be served with freshly baked homemade bread, salted pickles, and, according to Odilon, "a good drink of Caribou."*

Place **a piece of pork rind**** in a cast-iron pan, fat side of rind touching bottom of pan. Place a **4-lb. (2 kg) piece of pork shoulder** on top and surround with **a 2—3-lb. (1—1.3 kg) pork hock,** cut into 3 pieces. Cover with **2 large onions,** minced, **4-5 garlic cloves,** minced, **1 tbsp. (15 mL) coarse salt,** ½ **tsp. (2 mL) ground cloves,** ½ **tsp. (2 mL) savory.** Bake at 325°F. (160°C) for 2 hours, uncovered. There is no need to baste nor check the meat.

After 2 hours, add **2 cups (500 mL) hot water** and cook for another hour, covered this time.

When done, remove meat from pan, remove the bones, and break up the meat with 2 forks. Cut up the rind and hock into very small pieces. Add to the meat. Mix together and pour into a mold of your choice.

Place the pan in which the meat was cooked over direct heat and bring the cooking juice to boil, then add ½ **cup (125 mL) cold black** *or* **green tea.** Scrape the bottom and the sides of the pan, boil 1 minute, then pour over the meat. Cool. Cover and refrigerate. Unmold to serve.

---

*Caribou, a very potent drink, is a mixture of white wine and Dutch gin. In my grandmother's time, dandelion or bee wine was used.

**Ask your butcher for a piece of pork rind when purchasing the pork shoulder.

The Old Granny's "Cretons"
Les cretons de la vieille

La vieille was my great-grandmother. I am sure she learned this dish from her French Normandy ancestors, as it is almost the same as the French dish *rillettes*.

This is one of the many Cretons recipes, very old-fashioned, but still the most tasty. Serve as an appetizer, or as a light meal with homemade bread and cabbage salad. It is a large recipe, which can be easily halved, but it freezes well and keeps for 3 to 4 months. Let it thaw out overnight. I divide mine in small pâté jars.

Ask your butcher to grind together twice **3 lb. (1.35 kg) fresh pork steak** and 3 lb. (1.35 kg) pork shank, and to grind separately **1½ lb. (750 g) leaf lard.**

Melt the leaf lard over low heat until only very small brown pieces remain, floating in the fat.

To this melted fat add the ground meat, **2 large onions,** minced, 2½ tbsp. (37 mL) coarse salt, ½ tsp. (5 mL) pepper, 4 cups (1 L) water, 1 tsp. (2 mL) ground cloves, 1 tsp. (5 mL) cinnamon, 1 tbsp. (15 mL) savory, 3 crushed garlic cloves. Cook slowly, uncovered, for 2 hours or until the liquid reduces to the level of the meat. **Add 2 cups (500 mL) dry bread-crumbs** (this absorbs excess fat). Stir for 5 minutes. Taste for seasoning, then pour into small bowls. Cover. Refrigerate or freeze.

Pork Roast Gravy
Sauce du rôti de porc

A Breton woman, who lived with my grandparents for many years, taught the women in the area how to make pork roast gravy, the way it was prepared in her Bretagne.

When the roast of pork is cooked, and you have some pea soup or some bean soup, here is what to do. Remove from the soup, with a perforated spoon, **1 cup (250 mL) beans** *or* peas, *mash them, and use to thicken the roast gravy. Add* **a pinch of ground cloves and sage.** *This is very, very good !*

I keep part of the gravy to make some graisse de rôti *(pork jelly). How can one improve on this!*

Tasty Economical Way to Use Leftover Ham
Manière économique de finir le jambon

Whenever Grand-mére served ham loaf, it was accompanied by a big bowl of buttered parsleyed (no cheese) noodles. Dessert was always dried fruits and whole nuts in a deep blue bowl (which I now have), with a nutcracker in the middle. For the grown-ups, there was a bottle of dry Madeira or port.

Ham bone — make pea soup.

Rind — make delicious cracklings. Cut it into squares, place on a baking sheet and brown in a 400°F. (200°C) oven for about 1 hour. When the rind is nice and crisp, break it up into pieces and serve for supper, with hot bread, or add to pea soup, or to a meat pie.

Cooled melted fat — make delicious flaky dough, to use with meat pie.

Leftover ham — chop up the bits and pieces very finely and mix them with **1 cup (250 mL) crushed dried bread** (for 2 cups [500 mL] of meat). Add **1 cup (250 mL) milk** beaten with **1 egg** and **1 tbsp. (15 mL) mustard.** Place in bread pan and top with a little **ham fat** *or* **butter.** Bake 30 minutes in a 325°F. (160°C) oven. A delicious ham loaf, hot or cold, and quite economical.

Fowl

Maple Syrup Broilers
Poussins au sirop d'érable (pour la visité)

This was a dish for company, and always a source of discussion between my grandparents as they had to decide which of the chickens ready for choosing were the most tender. I still have the old earthenware dish my grandmother used, and I often (not just for company) make this delicious casserole.

Quarter **2 very tender young broilers.** Roll each piece in **flour** seasoned with **salt** and **pepper.** Brown in **4 tbsp. (60 mL) butter.** Place the chicken pieces, as they are browned, in an attractive ovenproof earthenware dish.

Add **2 large thinly sliced onions** to the fat in the frying pan, brown, and pour on top of the chicken. **Salt** and **pepper.** Sprinkle with **a pinch of aniseed and savory** and pour **1 tbsp. (15 mL) maple syrup** over each piece of chicken.

Deglaze the frying pan with ½ **cup (125 mL) cider** *or* **water** and pour over the chicken. Bake 40 minutes, uncovered, in a 350°F. (180°C) oven.

Old Québec Boiled Dinner
Bouilli d'été de Grand-mère

As far back as I can remember, our family greeted the arrival of summer with "Old Québec Boiled Dinner."

Grandfather made his rounds in the garden every morning, watching for the arrival of the first string beans. He thinned the carrots and gathered the first small onions. When he returned with his basket filled with these tender young vegetables, we knew that the summer boiled dinner was on its way to the supper table, and that Grandfather would spend some time looking over his chickens before choosing the very best and the most plump. Meanwhile, Grandmother would choose a nice piece of salt pork, with some lean and some fat, from the large earthenware crock covered with a linen cloth.

Remove fat from **a 5–6 lb. (2.5–3 kg) stewing chicken.** Chop this fat and melt it in a soup kettle, over low heat. Rub the chicken skin vigorously with a whole nutmeg *or* ½ **tsp. (2 mL) grated nutmeg.** Then rub with **3 tbsp. (50 mL) brandy** *or* **cider vinegar. Salt** and **pepper** the chicken cavity and sprinkle with ½ **tsp. (2 mL) thyme** *or* **savory.**

Brown the chicken on all sides in the melted fat. Add a **2-lb. (1 kg) piece salt pork, 3 quarts (3 L) boiling water, 1 tbsp. (15 mL) coarse salt, ¼ tsp. (1 mL) savory, 2 large minced onions,** ½ **cup (125 mL) celery leaves,** finely chopped. Cover and simmer until chicken and pork are tender, about 1½ to 2 hours.

Half an hour before the end of the cooking period, add **1 new cabbage,** cut in 4 or 8 sections, **8–12 new carrots, 8–12 small whole onions, 2 lb. (1 kg) strir g beans** (tied together in small bundles with heavy thread), **1ʐ new potatoes.** Cover.

Bring back to boil, then cook slowly until vegetables are tender, about 20 minutes.

To serve, place the chicken and the salt pork in the middle of a large dish. Surround with the vegetables and serve with a sauceboat of "Grandmother's butter."

Melt ½ **cup (125 mL) butter,** add **3 tbsp. brandy** *or* **lemon juice,** ½ **cup (125 mL) chopped fresh parsley, ¼ cup (60 mL) chopped chives** *or* **green onions.**

Chicken Galantine
La galantine de poulet

The secret of success to this super jellied chicken is to make sure that the cup (250 mL) of water has completely evaporated when the chicken is cooked. If not, uncover and boil quickly until the water evaporates; then the warm cream binds it all together. I also add ½ tsp. (2 mL) tarragon to the water. Thyme is also pleasant, if you prefer it to tarragon.

Cut up in pieces **a 3–4 lb. (1.5–2 kg) chicken** and brown in **butter.** Remove to another pan. Slice **2 onions** thinly, place over chicken, and add **salt** and **pepper.** Deglaze the frying pan used to brown the chicken with **1 cup (250 mL) water,** pour over chicken, then cover the pan and simmer until tender, about 1 hour. Reserve the pan juices. Cool the chicken, then remove skin and bones. Chop the skin in the meat grinder or cut it up finely with a large knife. Chop the chicken meat coarsely, mix it with the skin, and place in a dish.

Add **1 cup (250 mL) rich cream** to the pan juices and heat without boiling. Pour over the chicken and let set overnight in a cold place. After 24 hours, the delicious chicken is coated with a nice ivory jelly.

If you don't wish to add the shredded cooked skin (extra calories), omit it, but don't remove it before cooking the chicken, as it is important in forming the gelatinous matter.

Chicken Fricassée with Dumplings
Fricassée de poulet d'Olivine,
servie avec 'Grands-pères' ou 'Glissantes'

Olivine was my paternal grandmother's name. In the old days, only French-Canadian women cooked dumplings in sauce, dumplings being the influence of English cooking. They never called them dumplings, but *glissantes,* which means "slippery," most likely because of their appearance. I have never found a better recipe for dumplings — light, tasty, and quick — and nowadays, I make them in the microwave.

Cut up **a 4–6 lb. (2–3 kg) chicken** into individual pieces. Brown the pieces in a little **butter** *or* **fat** (the best is melted chicken fat).

When all the pieces are browned, cover sparingly with **boiling water,** add **2 tsp. (10 mL) salt, 1 carrot, 1 onion, 3 stems parsley, 1 whole clove, 2 garlic cloves, 1 bay leaf, ½ tsp. (1 mL) thyme.** Cover and cook until chicken is tender, about 40 minutes.

Prepare dumpling dough as follows. Sift together **2 cups (500 mL) all-purpose flour, 2 tbsp. (30mL) baking powder** (no error), **½ tsp. (2 mL) salt.** Add **2 eggs, 1 cup (250 mL) milk,** and beat until you have a light dough, adding milk, if necessary.

When the chicken is cooked, remove it from the liquid and keep in a warm place. Pour the dough by spoonfuls into the bouillon. Do not add more than 5 or 6 at a time. Cover immediately and boil 10 minutes. Remove the cooked dumplings and continue in this manner until all the dough is used. When the dumplings are cooked, you will have a delicious sauce to serve with the chicken.

Jiffy Chicken Liver Pâté
Pâté vite fait avec mes foies de volailles

Instead of putting the liver mixture through a meat chopper, I use my food processor or blender, both unknown to Grand-mère. I flavor the mixture with thyme or a few cloves of garlic, which I add when browning the livers. Keep the pâté refrigerated.

Grandmother browned **chicken livers** and **a sliced onion** in **butter** for 10 minutes. This was cooled slightly and passed through the meat grinder with **1–2 hard-boiled eggs** and **a bit of savory**. She then added **salt** and **pepper**, mixed it well, and poured the pâté into a small earthenware bowl.

It keeps well and is very good as a sandwich filling or as a *foie gras*.

The Perfect Way to Serve
Christmas Turkey
Manière facile de servir
la dinde de Noël

This recipe has saved me many last minute problems, as it is an ideal way to prepare a large turkey when serving many guests. Grand-mère kept the turkey in her cold kitchen and I keep mine in my cold pantry. It can also be refrigerated, as long as it is at room temperature 2 hours before reheating.

Potato Stuffing:
Beat 2 **eggs** until very light, add **2 cups (500 mL) milk,** and pour mixture over **4 cups (1 L) coarse dry breadcrumbs.** Add **1 tbsp. (15 mL) salt,** ½ **tsp. (2 mL) pepper,** 2 cups (500 mL) **mashed potatoes,** ½ **cup (125 mL) finely chopped celery.** Mix together.

Melt ¼ **cup (60 mL) butter,** add **1 large onion,** chopped, and brown over medium heat, 5 to 6 minutes. Add the stuffing and cook for approximately 10 minutes, stirring almost constantly. This amount is sufficient for **one 15-18 lb. (7-9 kg) turkey.**

Place the stuffing in a pan, leaving at least 1 inch (2.5 cm) of space from the top. Bake 30 minutes in a 350°F. (180°C) oven. Cool, cover, and refrigerate.

To Prepare Turkey:

Fill the cavity with **1 onion,** cut in 4, **1 stick celery,** cut in 3, **1 tsp. (2 mL) thyme, 1 tbsp. (15 mL) coarse salt,** ½ **tsp. (2 mL) pepper.**

Mix **1 tsp. (5 mL) dry mustard** with **4 tbsp. (60 mL) soft butter.** Spread all over the turkey and roast as usual.

Cool the roasted turkey and make the gravy. Pour a few spoonfuls of gravy over the stuffing and reserve the rest.

When the turkey has cooled, slice the white meat and place over half the pan of stuffing; cover the other half with the brown meat. Cover pan with foil and keep in a cool place.

The next day, 40 minutes before serving, pour a cupful (250 mL) of gravy all over the meat. Cover with foil. Heat in a 350°F. (180°C) oven 30 to 40 minutes. Serve.

Blue Grape Ketchup
Le ketchup aux raisins bleus

This very old recipe appears to have almost disappeared, as even Grandmother writes:

This wonderful ketchup recipe is almost lost, yet it is so good that I owe it to my daughters to write it down so it will not be forgotten.

Thanks to Grand-maman's foresight, it is my pleasure to give it to you now, so that your daughters will remember it.

Stem **5 pints (2.25L) blue Concord grapes** and place in an enamelled cast-iron saucepan over low heat, crushing them lightly to extract juice. Cook 20 to 25 minutes.

Pass through a fine sieve, pressing the pulp as much as possible. Add **4 cups (500 g) maple** *or* **brown sugar, 1 pint (500 mL) cider vinegar, 2 tbsp. (30 mL) each ground cinnamon and allspice, 1 tbsp. (15 mL) ground cloves, 1 tsp. (5 mL) freshly grated nutmeg, 1 tsp. (5 mL) coarse salt.** Boil approximately 45 minutes, or until the texture is correct. Stir often to prevent sticking.

Pour into sterilized jars and seal. Let stand 2 to 3 months. A perfect accompaniment for chicken, roast turkey, or lamb. *Yield: 2 pints (1 L).*

Leftover Turkey or Chicken Hash
La fricassée fatiguée

In days that followed Christmas, every bit of the turkey was used — the bones for soup, the skin, diced and crisped in the oven until browned, then served, instead of butter, on toasted homemade bread. So, when it came time to make hash from all the little bits and pieces, the children felt the poor turkey must be tired *(fatiguée)*, hence the name. I still like to make this turkey *fricassée* at least once every Christmas!

Heat in a frying pan 2–3 tbsp. (30–50 mL) **melted turkey** *or* **chicken fat** *or* **butter.** Add **1 large onion,** thinly sliced, and ½ **cup (125 mL) celery,** diced. Heat 5 to 8 minutes, over low heat, stirring often. Add **2–3 cups (500–750 mL) turkey.** Cook 5 minutes over low heat.

Make a sauce with **2 tbsp. (30 mL) turkey** *or* **chicken fat, 3 tbsp. (50 mL) flour, 2½ cups (625 mL) water.** Brown the fat and the flour well before adding the water. Add ½ **tsp. (2 mL) savory, salt** and **pepper** to taste. When the sauce is smooth and creamy, add ¼ **cup (60 mL) cream** and any remaining **turkey** *or* **chicken gravy.** Pour over the turkey or chicken. Simmer 15 minutes, then serve with hot biscuits and pickled beets.

Hot Biscuits (made with cream):
Sift together in a bowl **2 cups (500 mL) all-purpose flour, 1 tbsp. (15 mL) baking powder** (no error), **1 tsp. (5 mL) salt.** Mix together ¾ **cup (180 mL) rich cream** with **2 beaten eggs.** Add to the flour and mix just enough to moisten; the dough is rather soft and should remain lumpy. Stir as little as possible. Drop by spoonfuls onto a greased cookie sheet. Cook 15 minutes in a 400 °F. (200 °C) oven.

Stuffed Goose Neck
Cou d'oie farci

When I was studying in France in the Twenties, I often ate stuffed goose neck. I remember my surprise, when I discovered it there, since I thought it was my grandmother's creation.

I use the neck to make gravy for the roasted goose. Simmer the neck (withough the skin) in 1 cup (250 mL) water and ½ cup (125 mL) apple peels for 1 hour. Strain and use in the gravy. (Both the neck and liver can be frozen.)

To Stuff the Neck:
Thaw it out, then gently pull off the skin. Soak or marinate the unbroken skin in **water with vinegar** *or* in **wine**, enough to cover, and season with **salt, pepper, cinnamon, cloves.**

To Make the Stuffing:
Mix together, for each neck to be stuffed, ½ **lb. (250 g) sausage meat, 1 goose liver** (which I freeze with the neck), **1 garlic clove,** crushed, **1 tbsp. (15 mL) dried parsley, mace, salt,** and **pepper,** to taste. Add a few spoonfuls of the marinade used to soak the neck.

Tie the neck skin at one end with heavy thread, stuff with the mixture, and tie the other end. Brown the stuffed neck in **hot fat** *or* **butter.** Cover and let cook slowly over low heat for 1 hour.

When cooled, it is the best *saucisson* you can find. (One neck gives 1 lb. (500 g) of *saucisson.)*

Wild Duck Châteauguay
Canard sauvage de Châteauguay

During the hunting season, my grandfather would invite his friends for a duck dinner — Wild Duck Châteauguay — named by one of his good friends who lived in Châteauguay. This recipe was handed down from the friend's great-grandmother. The way in which recipes travel has never ceased to amaze me. For instance, if you live in the Lower St. Lawrence region, say Châteauguay, and pass this recipe on to your son, who moves to the Northwest Territories, then picture the distance travelled by this recipe which originated in what was at one time a little village. This is how table tradition is perpetuated; recipes do and must travel.

Clean **2 wild ducks; salt and pepper** the cavities. Place in a saucepan (my grandmother used cast-iron frying pan) and bake in a 425 °F. (215 °C) oven about 20 minutes per pound (500 g). Do not cover and do not add water. After 30 minutes, prick the duck legs with a knitting needle to release some of the fat. Continue cooking.

The day before cooking the duck make a Potato Water Bread. Remove a slice from the top of the loaf (reserve slice) and scoop out the crumbs with your fingers. Place the soft breadcrumbs in large pieces around the ducks. When they are browned and crisp, remove from pan, drain, and set on brown paper.

Remove the cooked ducks from the pan. Pour into the pan juices **4 cups (1 L) unpeeled apples,** thinly sliced, **½ tsp. (2 mL) cinnamon, 1 tbsp. (15 mL) brown sugar** *or* **maple syrup.** Cook on top of the stove until the apples are tender, about 15 minutes.

Place half the apples in the bottom of the scooped-out bread loaf. Cut the ducks in 4, set over the apples in the loaf, and top with remaining apples. Pour over all **1 cup (250 mL) hot cream** *or* **½ cup (125 mL) cream and ½ cup (125 mL) port wine** heated together. Replace the top slice and heat 30 minutes in a 325 °F. (160 °C) oven. This is a real treat!

The Trapper's Partridge
Perdrix du trappeur de "la Nord"

This delightful recipe came from an old trapper, "Martinquet," who used to come down "la Nord" River (as my grandmother wrote) every spring. She taught me to cook partridge his way.

Place **4 cups (500 g) each shredded cabbage and chopped onions** in a large wooden bowl and chop together until well mixed, so that each will absorb the other's flavor.

Add **2 lightly beaten eggs,** stir, then add about **1 cup (250 mL) cream** — just enough for a thick mixture. **Salt** and **pepper.** Clean **1–2 plump partridges** and stuff with a little of the cabbage-onion mixture. Sew up the cavities. Spread **soft butter** over each bird. Cover the breasts with slices of **salt pork.**

Butter a cast-iron frying pan generously. Set the partridges in the middle. Bake 30 to 40 minutes at 400°F. (200°C), uncovered. Baste often with melted butter. When the partridges have browned, place the remaining cabbage all around. Remove salt pork slices from the partridges and place on top of the cabbage. Cook for another 20 minutes, or more if necessary, until the partridges are tender.

Serve with baked potatoes and garnish with small pieces of salt pork, fried with a sliver of garlic, until brown and crisp.

Fish

Salmon Marinated in Vinegar
Saumon en marinade au vinaigre

Many fresh water fish can be marinated in this manner, and are delicious as a cool lunch dish. The following is my grandmother's method.

> *Cut the* **salmon** *in pieces and boil in water until tender, but do not overcook. Remove fish from water and add to the liquid* 1 **bay leaf, 10 peppercorns, 1 tbsp. (15 mL) coarse salt.** *Bring to the boil, measure water, and add an equal amount of the best vinegar. Place the salmon in an earthenware crock and cover with the marinade. Cover the crock with a clean linen cloth and let it marinate for a month before serving. Keep in the cold pantry.*

My method is to bring the water to a boil in a pan large enough to hold the whole fish (a 2 lb. [1 kg.] piece). Add a **thinly sliced unpeeled lemon** and 1 tsp. **(5 mL) pickling spices,** then boil for 5 minutes. Add the salmon and boil over medium heat 10 minutes per inch (2.5 cm) of thickness. This is important, as overcooking the fish will destroy its delicate flavor.

Measure 2 cups (500 mL) of the cooking water. Add **1 bay leaf** and **2 cups (500 mL) cider vinegar.** Bring to boil. Place the cooked salmon, cut in pieces, in a glass jar, then pour enough vinegar mixture on top to cover it completely. Seal. Refrigerate about 4 weeks before using.

How My Grandfather Cooked Trout
Manière de mon grand-père pour cuire les truites

The homemade dandelion wine in this recipe can be replaced by a dry white wine or dry cider, and the griddle by a cookie sheet.

Another extract from the little black book:

When returning from a trout fishing trip, my husband [my grandfather] always insists on cooking his own fish. This is his method:

He sprinkles the fish with **salt,** *inside and outside, places them in a large saucepan and sprinkles them with the* **juice of 2 lemons** *(for 6), or sometimes he covers them with our* **dandelion wine.** *Then he places the fish in the cold pantry to marinate for 1 hour. To cook the trout, he needs a large plate with some* **flour.** *He rolls each fish in the flour and sprinkles it with* **olive oil.** *He sets the trout on a griddle to cook 15 minutes in a 500°F. (250°C) oven, then serves them with a dandelion salad.*

The Ménard Brothers' Pickled Fish
Le poisson mariné des frères Ménard

The Ménard brothers were Indian fishing guides, friends of my grandfather. I remember them shooting the Lachine Rapids, standing up in the rowboat while harpooning the fish. Their pickled fish recipe is the best I've tasted.

In the early 1900s almost every home made its own dandelion or bee wine. I never liked the bee wine, because you could see little dead bees floating on top of the wine! A dry white wine can replace it.

Place in a saucepan ½ **cup (125 mL) cider vinegar, 2 cups (500 mL) dandelion** *or* **bee wine** (white Canadian wine may be used), **1 large onion**, thinly sliced, **1 sliced carrot, 2 tsp. (10 mL) coarse salt, a few whole cloves,** ¼ **tsp. (1 mL) thyme, 6 peppercorns,** ½ **tsp. (2 mL) celery seed.** Bring to boil and simmer 20 minutes, uncovered.

Clean the fish (for instance, 10—12 small trout or a 4-lb. (2 kg) salmon, sliced, may be used). Add to the boiled liquid and simmer 15–20 minutes, without boiling.

Carefully remove fish, so as not to break it, and place the pieces in a large glass jar. Cover with the cooking liquid. Serve well chilled, in the juice. Keeps for 3 to 5 weeks refrigerated and well covered.

Vegetables and Eggs

The Mother Superior's Cabbage Salad
La salade de choux de la Mère Supérieure

The Mother Superior at the village convent would prepare this recipe for special guests. Many people still make this cabbage salad with sour cream.

Mix together in a large bowl, **3 cups (750 mL) finely grated cabbage, 1 small onion,** minced, **½ tsp. (2 mL) salt, 2 unpeeled red apples,** grated.

Mix together **1 tbsp. (15 mL) sugar, 2 tbsp. (30 mL) vinegar, ¼ tsp. (1 mL) salt, ¼ tsp. (1 mL) pepper, ½ cup (125 mL) thick sour cream.**

Refrigerate the salad and dressing for 20 minutes before serving. Then pour the dressing over the cabbage, mix well, and taste for salt and vinegar.

Red Cabbage Duck
Choux rouges pour le canard

I replace the homemade *vin de cerises* by a semi-dry red wine or dry cider. I also use 4 medium apples instead of 2. Fresh pork fat is sometimes difficult to find nowadays; replace it with ½ lb. (227 g) fat bacon.

Marinate **2 cleaned ducks** *overnight in* **homemade cherry wine** *with a few spices.*

Mince about **4 cups (2 kg) red cabbage** *and add* **1 large onion,** *thinly sliced,* **2 unpeeled apples,** *grated,* **½ tsp. (2 mL) each cloves and cinnamon, 1 tsp. (5 mL) savory.** *Stuff the ducks very full with this mixture, and cook them 1 hour in the cast-iron Dutch oven lined with strips of fresh pork fat.*

Molded Cauliflower for Christmas Dinner
Choufleur pour le dîner de Noël

My Grandmother's cold cellar was a sight to behold. Square boxes were scattered all around the cool room, always neatly painted in white enamel, except for the bottoms. Red letters on a large wooden plaque indicated what vegetables each one contained. In just a few seconds you could read all the plaques and make your choice, then dig into the sand and take the vegetables you needed. Large bouquets of herbs, tied with strings of wool, hung on the wall and on top of the herbs were bottles and bottles of pickles, preserves, and so on.

The beautifully preserved autumn cauliflower — a must at every Christmas dinner — was steamed and generously topped with shredded homemade Cheddar and rich cream. (At that time, you could only have such luxury if you had a cold cellar.) It was also served cold (room temperature) when there was no time for last minute cooking.

Fill a saucepan with water and bring to boil. Add ¼ **tsp. (1 mL) sugar, a pinch of pepper, 1 peeled onion,** cut in 2, and bring back to boil. Then add **1 medium** *or* **2 small cauliflowers,** cut into flowerets, and boil uncovered until tender, about 20 minutes. Drain in a colander and rinse under cold running water. Drain again and mash. **Salt** and **pepper** and place in a round bowl, pushing cauliflower down with a spoon. Cover and refrigerate overnight. Mix the remaining ingredients together and refrigerate.

Stir ½ **cup (125 mL) mayonnaise** with the **grated rind and juice of ½ lemon,** and refrigerate. To serve, unmold the cauliflower and spread the dressing all over it. Sprinkle with ¼ **cup (60 mL) finely minced fresh parsley.**

Old-fashioned Dandelion Salad
La salade aux pissenlits des vieux

Grandmother served this salad with homemade cottage cheese and hot bread every year on the first day of May, as a salute to spring. The problem is not only picking the small, tender dandelion shoots, but also the long process of cleaning them. (Grandmother prepared one large earthenware bowl-ful.) Still, I find the enjoyment of eating this once-a-year salad worth the effort. Grandmother's recipe calls for salt pork, but it can be replaced by bacon.

Fry **6 slices salt pork** *or* **bacon** until brown and crisp; easily done over low heat in an enamelled cast-iron frying pan. Drain on paper.

Add **1 small onion,** chopped fine, and **3 tbsp. (50 ml) cider** *or* **wine vinegar** to the fat remaining in the pan. Bring to boil.

Remove from heat, let stand 1 minute, then pour over the dandelions. **Salt** and **pepper.** Add the fried salt and pork or mix well, and serve immediately.

A Tasty Way to Serve Canned Green Peas
Ses petits pois verts

Drain the liquid from a can of green peas into a saucepan. Add **1 small onion,** chopped fine, **1 tbsp. (15 mL) butter, a pinch of salt, a pinch of sugar, a little pepper.** Boil 10 minutes over high heat or until the liquid reduces to 3 tbsp. (50 mL). This can be done ahead of time.

Five minutes before serving, pour the drained peas into the very hot reduced liquid. Cover and heat 5 minutes over low heat. Serve.

Uncle Narcisse's Red Pickled Onions
Les oignons rouges marinés de mon oncle Narcisse

Uncle Narcisse, whose passion was hunting, was my grand-mother's brother. When he cooked his superb wild duck, my grandmother made delicious bread.

Every fall, this meal called for a family gathering and Uncle Narcisse was the "cock of the roost," as the elders said. He would bring along the cooked ducks, and onions for this salad, which was his recipe.

Peel **2–4 large red onions,** slice as thinly as possible, and break into rings. Slice **1 unpeeled lemon** very thinly.

Mix in a bowl ½ **tsp. (2 mL) salt,** ½ **cup (125 mL) olive oil,** ¼ **cup (60 mL) apple** *or* **cider vinegar,** the **juice of 1 lemon.** Add the onion rings and lemon slices. Mix thoroughly with a fork.

Cover and marinate at least 24 hours in the refrigerator. Serve with hot homemade bread and cold duck slices.

Small Pickled Onions
Les petits oignons marinés

I often make these just for the pleasure of biting into little pieces of pickled onions in my mashed potatoes. They can be easily purchased in bottles in grocery stores, as small onions for pickling are only available in autumn. Like Grand-mère, I use unsweetened pickled onions, but I also add a pinch of savory.

Oven-Baked Potatoes
Pommes de terre cuites au four

When I want to use potatoes for frying or boiling, I scrub them thoroughly with a brush, then peel them more thickly than usual. I wrap the peels in a cloth and keep them in a cool place. The next day I lightly butter each piece of peel, sprinkle salt and pepper, and set the peels on a cookie sheet, skin side up. I bake them 30 to 40 minutes in a 375°F. (190°C) oven. The hot crisp golden potato peels can be served as appetizers, or with a salad. Economical and delicious.

Rub potatoes with a piece of soft butter and roll them in coarse salt to give the peel a delicious flavor. Then bake them in a 400°F. (200°C) oven for 1 hour. Fifteen minutes before the end of the cooking period, prick them with the point of a knife to make them crisp.

To bake potatoes quickly, slice off the top and bottom of each potato and prick it with a fork.

Pumpkin Potatoes
Pommes de terre à la citrouille

Grand-mère was a wizard with pumpkin. Her mashed pumpkin potatoes and pumpkin french-fried chips were super. It's amazing how most of what we enjoyed in our youth remains a pleasure as we grow older.

In the autumn of 1959 I made these on my TV show. The amount of mail requesting the recipe was unbelievable!

Boil together an equal quantity of **peeled potatoes** and **pumpkin.** When cooked, drain them, add **1 good-sized onion,** finely chopped, and **a piece of butter.** Mash it all until creamy, season to taste, and serve with golden slices of fried salt pork or bacon.

Rosana's Potato Omelet
Omelette aux patates de Rosana

My grandmother (Rosana) prepared this omelet on Friday for supper, as did my mother in our own home, and they served it with pickled gherkins and cabbage salad. Then it became my turn to make it.

The Québec English served hashed brown potatoes on the side with their omelet, but the French preferred them the following way.

Peel and slice very thinly **2** *or* **3 potatoes.** Peel and slice **2 medium-sized onions.** Melt **4 tbsp. (60 mL) bacon fat** in a frying pan. Add the potatoes and onions. Cook over quite high heat until the potatoes are cooked and golden brown.

Beat **6 eggs,** add ¼ **cup (60 mL) milk, salt** and **pepper,** ¼ **tsp. (1 mL) savory.** Pour over the potatoes and cook as an omelet. Serve immediately.

Eglantine's Chili Sauce
La sauce chili d'Eglantine

Eglantine was 18 years old when she first came to my grandmother's from her village of St-Rémi. From then on, for 31 years, she came every autumn for two months to make preserves and pickles. Many of the recipes in Grandmother's notebook were Eglantine's; a few of them are included in this book.

The walls of the cold cellar were lined all around with white shelves, that were scrubbed to a finish before the new season's goodies were placed on them. The floor was hard-beaten earth, topped with straw, which was supposed to keep the cold cellar cool and free from smell. In the middle of the large room stood a long white table on which the jars and bottles were placed for labelling. They were then set in their respective places on the shelves. About 200 to 300 jars and bottles were kept there, to be enjoyed until the next season. The door of the cellar was always locked, but I never knew why.

Scald **12 ripe red tomatoes.** Let stand 2 minutes. Drain, then place in cold water. Peel the tomatoes and chop in small pieces. Remove seeds and ribs of **4 green peppers** and cut in small pieces. Peel and chop finely **2 onions.** Peel and cut **4 apples** into thin slices.

Place in a large kettle the tomatoes, green peppers, onions, apples; add 2½ **cups (625 mL) light brown sugar, 1 pint (0.5 L) cider vinegar, 2 tbsp. (30 mL) coarse salt, 1 tsp. (5 mL) dry mustard, 1 tsp. (5 mL) celery seed, ½ tsp. (2 mL) ground cloves, ½ tsp. (2 mL) whole allspice, 1 tbsp. (15 mL) ground cinnamon, ¼ tsp. (1 mL) cayenne pepper.** Mix well.

Bring to the boil over medium heat, stirring a few times. Then cook over medium heat for 2 hours, or until mixture has thickened and become transparent.

Pour into sterilized jars. Seal. This quantity should yield approximately 4 pints (2 L) of chili sauce.

The Baker's Baked Beans
Les fèves au lard du boulanger

How I remember the baker's baked beans. They were so flavorful and fragrant, plump and golden, as they appeared piping hot on the breakfast table on Saturday morning, to everyone's delight! In the old days in Québec, it was customary to have the beans baked in the bread oven of the local baker or in the outdoor brick oven, after the bread had finished baking and the oven was cooling off.

Sort **4 cups (1 L) dried beans,** wash them, and soak overnight in cold water. The following morning heat the beans and their water over low heat and bring slowly to boil. Then simmer *(do not boil)* for 1 to 1¼ hours, until some of the beans' skins lift when blowing on them (this is an old foolproof trick which will indicate whether the beans are ready for the bean pot).

When the skins lift, drain the beans and reserve the water. Pour 1 cup (250 mL) of the water into the bean pot, well greased with a piece of salt pork. (I sometimes heat the bean pot in the oven for a few minutes, so that the fat will melt more readily when greasing it.) Then add half the beans, place on top **1 whole large red onion,** peeled and rolled in **1 tsp. (5 mL) dry mustard.** Add the remaining beans to almost fill the pot.

Make incisions in **a 1-1½ lb. (450-680 g) piece of salt pork** (lean and fat) and partially bury it in the beans. It can also be sliced thinly and placed at random in the beans, but it is tastier when buried in one piece.

Mix together **2 cups (500 mL) brown sugar,** ⅓-⅔ **cup (80-160 mL) molasses, 1 tbsp. (15 mL) salt,** and pour over the beans. Add the rest of the cooking water, and more hot water if necessary, to fill the pot. Some of the salt pork should show above the water. Cover and cook in a 300°F. (150°C) oven for at least 8 hours. Check the beans now and then to make sure there is juice simmering on top. If necessary, add a little hot water.

Beans are usually placed in the oven in the morning and eaten at night. They can also be baked in the early evening after supper, so they can still be watched, and served in the morning. In this case, once they are cooked by late evening, turn off the heat and let them stand in the oven. In the morning, they will still be warm and truly delicious.

Pickled Eggs
Les oeufs dans le vinaigre

Grandmother always added 1 garlic clove and 1 branch of savory to each jar. I do the same, to add a special touch to the eggs.

Make a small cotton bag and place in it **1 tsp. (5 mL) whole cloves, 1 tsp. (5 mL) peppercorns, ½ tsp. (2 mL) celery seed.** Put it in **3 cups (750 mL) white vinegar;** add **1½ cups (375 mL) water** and **1½ tsp. (8 mL) salt.** Bring to boil and continue boiling for 10 minutes; then cool.

Place **12 eggs** in a saucepan and cover with cold water, at least 1 inch (2.5 cm) above the eggs. Do not cover; bring to boil over high heat. As soon as the water reaches the fast boiling point, remove from heat and let stand 15 minutes. Pour into a bowl of ice water and shell the eggs immediately.

Place eggs in glass jars. Top with the cooled vinegar. Cover and keep in a cool place.

If you wish to have red eggs, use the vinegar from pickled beets, following the same recipe.

Cakes and Cookies

The Indian Woman's Cake
Gâteau de la sauvagesse

This was the specialty of an Indian woman who worked for my grandmother in the vegetable garden. The only cooking she did at Grandmother's was this cake, which was so delicious that she was often asked to make it. I have never seen this recipe anywhere else; the Indian woman said it came from her ancestors, and that the "good nuns" had taught them to make it. It may be true — it is a divine cake!

Cream ½ cup (125 mL) butter *or* bacon fat; add 1 cup (250 mL) white sugar, 1 cup (250 mL) brown sugar, 2 beaten eggs. Beat until you have a light mixture. Add 1 cup (250 mL) cooked puréed pumpkin (canned pumpkin may be used).

Sift together 3 cups (750 mL) pastry flour, 4 tsps. (20 mL) baking powder, ¼ tsp. (1 mL) baking soda, 1 tsp. (5 mL) ginger, ¼ tsp. (1 mL) cinnamon.

Gradually add the flour mixture to the creamed mixture, alternating with ½ cup (125 mL) milk. Blend in 1 cup (250 mL) chopped nuts (black walnuts were used) and 1 tsp. (5 mL) maple extract.

Grease 3 round 8-inch (20 cm) cake pans. Divide the dough between the pans. Bake 30 to 40 minutes at 350°F. (180°C). Let stand 10 minutes. Unmold on cake racks.

When the cakes have cooled, spread each layer with whipped cream flavored with maple extract, stack the layers, and sprinkle the top with finely chopped nuts.

49

Salt Pork Cake
Gâteau au lard salé

When eggs became scarce during the winter, Grandmother often made this cake, which is really "our very own." Before finding her little notebook, I didn't know that she added brandy to the recipe; after doing the same, I realized why my version had not tasted quite like Grandmother's. This cake will keep 3 to 4 months, well wrapped, in a cool place.

Pass through the meat grinder **1 lb. (500 g) salt pork fat** *or* **fresh pork fat** (no meat, just fat).

Scald the fat with **2 cups (500 mL) boiling water**. Add **2 tsp. (10 mL) soda, 2 cups (500 mL) sugar, 1 tsp. (5 mL) ground cloves, 1 cup (250 mL) molasses, 1 tsp. (5 mL) ginger, 2 tsp. (10 mL) cinnamon, 1 whole nutmeg**, grated, **1 lb. (500 g) currants, 1 lb. (500 g) raisins, 1 cup (250 mL) candied fruit peels, 1 cup (250 mL) chopped nuts, ½ cup (125 mL) brandy, 4 cups (1 L) all-purpose flour**. Mix together.

Pour batter into a loaf pan which has been lined with buttered brown paper. Bake 2 hours in a 350°F. (180°C) oven or until well done.

Aunt Octavie's Cornbread
Le pain de maïs dans le poêlon de fer d'Octavie

My aunt Octavie was the perfect Victorian character. She only wore long black dresses with white collars and cuffs. In the morning, it was a dress of shiny cotton and white linen; in the afternoon and evening, heavy silk taffeta and white lace; at Christmas and on other important holidays or events, she would dress in black velvet trimmed with handmade écru lace. The dresses were always identical, whatever the material. I will never forget the "frou-frou" sound as she walked around in her taffeta dress.

No one ever saw her working in the kitchen. It was not "ladylike," according to her, but her food was always good and her table beautifully set. Octavie often served many types of hot breads, such as this cornbread, baked and served in her cast-iron pan (which I still use!). An Indian girl from Caughnawaga had woven a beautiful basket lined in bark, which just fitted the iron pan. To slice the bread, my aunt always used a long, sharp steel knife with the word "home" carved in the maple handle. I sometimes wonder if there are still such women in today's world!

Beat **1 cup (250 mL) milk** and **1 egg** together for a few moments.

Sift together **1⅓ cups (330 mL) cornflour**, **⅓ cup (80 mL) all-purpose flour**, **2 tbsp. (30 mL) sugar**, **1 tsp. (5 mL) salt**, **3 tsp. (15 mL) baking powder**. Add the milk and egg mixture to the dry ingredients. Stir just enough to mix.

Melt **2 tbsp. (30 mL) butter** in a cast-iron frying pan until nutty brown in colour. Pour in the dough and cover with **1 cup (250 mL) cold milk**. Do not stir. Cook 1 hour in a 350°F. (180°C) oven. Serve hot or warm with molasses or maple syrup.

My Aunt Poupée's Gingerbread
Le pain d'épices de Poupée

Poupée, as she was nicknamed, was the youngest of my grandmother's five sisters. I never knew the reason for that name, which she lived with all her life; perhaps it was because she made dolls for all the children, which amused us for many hours. We knew that come birthdays or Christmas, we would receive a doll from "Tante Poupée," or clothes to dress the ones we already had.

Poupée did very little cooking, as she never married. She spent her time visiting her sisters, staying a month here and a few days there. The one thing she made to perfection was what she called her gingerbread; in reality it is a honey cake.

Mix together in a bowl **1 cup (250 mL) sugar, ¾ cup (180 mL) clear honey, 2½ tsp. (12 mL) soda, ¼ tsp. (1 mL) salt.**

Brew **1 tsp. (5 mL) black** *or* **green tea in 1¼ cups (310 mL) boiling water.** Let steep 5 minutes, then pour over the sugar and honey. Stir to melt the sugar. Add **3 tbsp. (50 mL) rum, 1 tsp. (5 mL) aniseed, 2 tsp. (10 mL) cinnamon.**

Sift **4 cups (1 L) all-purpose flour.** Gradually add the flour to the liquid mixture, beating vigorously and constantly, until you have a smooth dough. Use only enough flour to obtain a soft smooth dough.

Pour into a buttered mold (which should have a capacity of 6 cups [1.5 L] liquid). Bake 10 minutes in a 450°F. (230°C. oven. Then lower heat to 350°F. (180°C) and bake 1 hour, or until the middle is well done.

Cool on a cake rack and unmold. When completely cooled, wrap in foil paper and keep in a cool place or in a plastic box. This gingerbread will keep 3 to 4 months. It is delicious served with sweet butter and honey, or simply as is with a good cup of tea.

Grandmother's Gingerbread Mix
Le pain d'épices dans le pot

Grandmother always had a gingerbread mix on hand so she could make it quickly. Cake mixes are not new, as you can see, but in those days homemakers made their own.

Grandmother had many variations for her gingerbread. Whenever she made one, it hardly had time to reach the table before it was all gone. Its French name derives from the fact that she would say, "Tonight I shall make *un pain d'épices dans le pot.*" The earthenware *pot* was a large, deep brown casserole where she kept the mix.

Grandmother's Ready-Mix
Sift carefully together twice in a large bowl **8 cups (2 L) all-purpose flour, 2¼ cups (560 mL) sugar, 2½ tsps. (12 mL) soda, 2 tbsp. (30 mL) baking powder, 3 tbsp. (50 mL) ground ginger, 3 tbsp. (50 mL) cinnamon, 1 tsp. (5 mL) cloves, 1 tbsp. (15 mL) salt.**

Measure **2¼ cups (560 mL) lard** *or* **vegetable shortening**, and cut it in the flour with 2 knives, until texture is mealy. Place in a metal box or an earthenware crock with a good lid. Store in a cool place or refrigerate; it keeps for 3 months. This is enough dough for 6 gingerbreads, 8 x 8 x 2 inches (20 x 20 x 5 cm) each.

Anise Gingerbread (Le pain d'épices à l'anis)
Measure **2 cups (500 mL) ready mix** and place in a bowl.

Mix together **1 beaten egg, ¼ tsp. (1 mL) aniseed, ½ cup (125 mL) molasses, ½ cup (125 mL) boiling water**. Add half this mixture to the ready mix. Stir and add the remaining mixture. Blend thoroughly. Pour into a greased pan. Bake 35 minutes in a 350°F. (180°C) oven.

Christmas Morning Gingerbread (Pain d'épices du déjeuner de Noël)
Prepare the **ready mix** the same way as for the Anise Gingerbread; but add **1 cup (250 mL) mincemeat** before adding the liquid mixture. Bake 50 minutes in a 350°F. (180°C) oven.

"Sugaring Party" Gingerbread (Pain d'épices pour les "parties de sucre")
Place in a bowl **2 cups (500 mL) ready mix**. Heat ⅔ **cup (160 mL) maple syrup**; mix with ⅓ **cup (80 mL) sour cream**, pour over the mix, stir together, and add **1 beaten egg**. Bake 40 minutes in a 350°F. (180°C) oven.

Maple Syrup "Tourlouche"
La tourlouche au sirop d'érable

During the spring sap period, many people still bake a "tourlouche." My grandmother used to make 50 to 75, to serve at the sugaring house. All-purpose flour can be used in equal quantity to replace whole wheat flour. It is a light dessert, even when made with whole wheat flour. Cover it well during baking.

Boil **1 cup (250 mL) maple syrup** for 5 minutes. Remove from heat and pour into an 8-inch (20 cm) cake pan.

Beat together **1 tbsp. (15 mL) butter, 3 tbsp. (50 mL) maple sugar** *or* **white sugar, 1 egg**, until you have a creamy mixture.

Sift together **1 cup (250 mL) whole wheat flour, 2 tsp. (10 mL) baking powder**, ¼ **tsp. (1 mL) salt**, ½ **tsp. (2 mL) nutmeg**. Gradually add to the egg mixture, alternating with ½ **cup (125 mL) milk** and **1 tsp. (5 mL) vanilla**. Pour over the syrup. Cover and bake 25 minutes at 400°F. (200°C).

Unmold and sprinkle with chopped nuts. Serve warm with whipped cream or as is.

Currant Cakes
Gâteau raisin de corinthe

Late in June, Grandmother would make rosewater from the hundreds of wild roses she had around her house. She used distilled water and fresh rose petals. Some of the rosewater was for beauty care — the custom was to rub your face with it every morning — but a bottle or two was also kept in the kitchen for flavoring.

The first strawberries of the season were always served with fine sugar and a few drops of rosewater. These currant cookies were also flavored with it, to serve at teatime. Few people can tell what the intriguing flavor is.

Cream together until fluffy **1 cup (250 mL) soft butter** and **1 cup (250 mL) sugar** (I beat it in my mixer for 10 minutes). Add **3 eggs**, one at a time, beating 3 minutes between each egg. Add **1 tbsp. (15 mL) rosewater**, and beat 40 seconds.

Mix **2 cups (500 mL) flour** with ½ **tsp. (2 mL) baking powder**; stir in ½ cup (125 mL) currants. Add to creamed mixture and beat just enough to mix. Drop by spoonfuls on a greased cookie sheet. Sprinkle lightly with sugar.

Bake in a 375 °F. (190 °C) oven for 12 to 14 minutes, or until golden brown around the edges. Cool on a wire rack.

Small Economical Cookies
Petites galettes pas chères

When we visited our grandmother, she always had a jar of nourishing crispy little cookies. A recipe of my great-grandmother's — she placed all the ingredients in a bowl and mixed them, then dropped the mixture by spoonfuls on a cookie sheet.

The ingredients are as follows: **1 cup (250 mL) all-purpose flour, 1 cup (250 mL) brown sugar** *(for Jehane, I sometimes make them with maple syrup)* [I see that my grandmother knew what I liked!] ½ **tsp. (2 mL) baking soda,** ½ **tsp. (2 mL) salt, 3 cups (375 mL) oatmeal,** ¾ **cup (200 mL) bacon** *or* **chicken fat,** ½ **cup (125 mL) sour cream** *or* **milk**. *I cook the biscuits in a 350 °F. (180 °C) oven.*

I also add ½ tsp. (2 mL) freshly grated nutmeg *and* ½ tsp. (2 mL) allspice *to the flour. I sometimes replace 1 cup (250 mL) of the oatmeal by* 1 cup (250 mL) wheat germ. *Another variation that I enjoy is adding* ¼ cup (60 mL) chopped walnuts *or* seedless raisins. *Try them; they are tasty!*

Pink Sugar Cookies
Biscuits au sucre rose

The children always said to my grandmother, "You never make your cookies large enough." She gave the cookies with the most pink sugar to the well-behaved children; to the others she gave the cookies in the bottom of the jar, which always seemed to have lost some of their pink sugar.

Grandmother made her own pink sugar the old-fashioned way. She cooked 1 sliced beet in ½ cup (125 mL) water. When the water was nice and red, she strained and cooled it. To prepare the sugar, she poured a few drops of this dye over granulated sugar until she had the desired color. To tint the sugar she would manipulate it with her fingertips.

Cream lightly ½ cup (125 mL) butter, ½ cup (125 mL) lard *or* bacon fat *or* shortening. Add 1 cup (250 mL) sugar and mix thoroughly. Add 1 cup (250 mL) sour cream, 3 beaten egg yolks, 1 tsp. (5 mL) vanilla. Beat together until you have a light cream.

Sift together 3 cups (750 mL) all-purpose flour, 1 tsp. (5 mL) salt, 1 tsp. (5 mL) baking powder, ½ tsp. (2 mL) baking soda, 1 tsp. (5 mL) crushed anise seeds. Add gradually to the creamed mixture for a light dough. The lighter the dough the crispier the cookies. Let stand 1 hour in the refrigerator.

Divide the dough into 3 balls. Roll each ball on a lightly floured board to about ⅛ inch (0.3 cm) thickness. Cut with a glass or a 2½-inch (7.75 cm) cookie cutter. Place on a buttered cookie sheet. Sprinkle with pink sugar to taste. Bake 10 to 15 minutes in a 375°F. (190°C) oven.

Pies

Company Apple Pie
La tarte aux pommes de la visite

My grandmother, like many women of her time, made good Canadian cheese — both mild and old — fresh white cheese similar to cottage cheese. The Italian women who immigrated in large numbers in the early 1900s taught the Québec women how to make Ricotta, which is Italian cottage cheese. My grandmother would often make her apple pie with layers of apples and cottage cheese, using some sweetening and spicing. As they were big fat pies, baked in deep earthenware or tin pie plates, it was necessary to tie cotton around the crust. Nowadays, we use fewer apples in our pies, so the juice does not run all over; also, cleaning a woodstove oven was no small chore.

Line a pie plate with **a crust of your choice**.

Slice **peeled apples** directly into the plate, piling them quite high in the middle. As you fill the plate, dot here and there with **1 tbsp. (15 mL) butter** cut into small pieces. Mix together **½ tsp. (2 mL) cinnamon, ½ tsp. (2 mL) nutmeg, rind of ½ lemon, a pinch of salt, ¾ cup (180 mL) maple *or* brown sugar**, and sprinkle over the apples. Squeeze the **juice of 1 lemon** on top.

Cover with **a crust**. To prevent the juice from spilling over in the oven, dip a 1 inch (2.5 cm) strip of cotton in milk and tie it all around the crust (aluminum foil can replace the cotton). Remove from crust 20 minutes before the end of the cooking period.

Bake the pie 15 minutes in a 425°F. (215°C) oven. Lower heat to 325°F. (160°C) and bake another 50 minutes. Serve with a wedge of Cheddar or other cheese of your choice.

Dried Apple Pie
Tarte aux pommes sèches

Often in the autumn we would sit around Grandmother while she peeled, cored, and cut rounds of apples, which we then ran through thick linen thread. There had to be 30 to a string — what fun we had counting them. Then they were hung in the cool summer kitchen to dry. In the winter I remember eating hot porridge with pieces of dried apples cooked in it. At New Year's dinner, Dried Apple Pie was a must.

Soak **3–4 cups (750–1000 mL) dried apples** in **1 cup (250 mL) Scotch whiskey** *or* **strong cider**. Then mix them with ½ **cup (125 mL) each molasses and honey, 1 tsp. (5 mL) ground ginger, ½ tsp. (2 mL) mace.** Stir well, and pour into **an unbaked pastry shell.** Dot with **butter** here and there, then bake in a 400°F. (200°C) oven, about 30 minutes.

The pie never had a top crust and cooked rather flat. It was served covered with a thick layer of sweetened whipped cream.

Toinon's Sour Cream Apple Pie
La tarte aux pommes de Toinon (à la crème sure)

My mother's sister Toinon (short for Antoinette) preferred to cook only desserts, which she made to perfection.

Line a 9-inch (22.5 cm) pie plate with **pastry of your choice.**

Slice enough **peeled apples** to fill the plate generously. Add ½ **cup (125 mL) brown sugar.** Mix with a fork and set aside.

Beat together in a bowl **1 egg, 2 cups (500 mL) sour cream, ½ cup (125 mL) brown sugar, 2 tbsp. (30 mL) flour, ½ tsp. (2 mL) cinnamon, a pinch each nutmeg, cloves, salt.**

Pour half this mixture over the pastry, cover with the sliced apples, then top with the remaining mixture. Bake at 400°F. (200°C) for 45 to 60 minutes or until browned. Cool and serve. The top of this single-crust pie is nicely browned and the inside is creamy.

Clarissa's Blue Grape Pie
La tarte aux raisins bleus de Clarissa

Clarissa was my grandmother's cook for 35 years! She rarely spoke, but was always smiling. She loved roses and forget-me-nots, and in the summer Grand-mère always made a bouquet of both for her room.

Wash and remove from their clusters **3 cups (750 mL) Concord blue grapes.** Press each grape to remove the pulp. Put the skins aside and heat the pulp. When it reaches boiling point, remove from heat and strain, pressing hard, to remove the seeds.

Mix the grape skins with **1½ cups (375 mL) sugar, 3 tbsp. (50 mL) flour, a pinch of salt, a little lemon rind.** Add the pulp and mix thoroughly.

Pour the mixture into a 9-inch pie plate lined with **pastry of your choice.** Cover with **a full crust** *or* **a lattice.** Bake 10 minutes in a 450°F. (230°C) oven. Then lower heat to 350°F. (180°C) and bake 30 minutes.

Mélanie's Black Walnut Caramel Pie
La tarte au caramel et aux noix longues de Mélanie

After the black walnuts had been picked in the fall, the men would sit by the fire in the evening and crack them on the back of an iron with a hammer. In those days, irons were made of black iron and heated on top of the stove.

Prepare two 9-inch (22.5 cm) pie plates. Line with **pastry of your choice.** Keep refrigerated until ready to use.

Beat **4 eggs** until frothy and light.

Melt **3 tbsp. (50 mL) butter** and add to the beaten eggs along with **1⅓ cups (320 mL) maple syrup, 1⅓ cups (320 mL) brown sugar,** well packed, **a pinch of salt.** Mix well.

Sift **3 tbsp. (50 mL) all-purpose flour** over the egg mixture. Add **1 tsp. (5 mL) vanilla** and beat with a rotary beater until it has a smooth consistency. Add **1 cup (250 mL) nuts,** chopped coarsely, and divide the mixture between the 2 pie plates.

Do not cover with pastry. Bake 20 to 25 minutes in a 375°F. (190°C) oven.

Spring Rhubarb Pie
La tarte rose du printemps

Mother made this pie for my sister's First Communion dinner. She topped the crust with thinly slivered almonds and a few crushed macaroons before baking it. It was served warm, with whipped cream. A delicious and attractive way to make a simple rhubarb pie.

Mix together **2½ cups (750 mL) garden rhubarb,** diced, **¾ cup (180 mL) sugar, 2½ tbsp. (40 mL) cream of wheat, 1 tsp. (5 mL) each lemon juice and grated lemon rind, a pinch nutmeg, a pinch salt.** Let stand 15 minutes. Add **2–3 cups (500–750 mL) strawberries,** left whole. Stir lightly.

Pour the mixture into a baking dish, dot with a few pats of **butter,** and top with **pie crust of your choice.** Bake 30 minutes at 400°F. (200°C) or until pastry is golden brown.

Vinegar Pie
Tarte au vinaigre

Grandmother's recipe simply listed the ingredients, without measurements, in the belief that everyone knew just how much to use. This pie dates back to the English colonial days.

We children called it "the shaky pie," because when cooled, the inside quivered like gelatine when the pie was moved. This recipe gives 6 to 8 large servings.

Beat **4 egg yolks** until very light. Beat **2 egg whites** until stiff. Fold **1 cup (250 mL) sugar** into the beaten egg whites, then beat to the consistency of a meringue. Fold this meringue into the beaten egg yolks.

Sift together ¼ **cup (60 mL) flour,** ½ **tsp. (2 mL) each nutmeg, cinnamon, allspice, cloves, a little salt**. Add the spice and flour mixture to the egg mixture, alternating with **1 cup (250 mL) sour cream**. When thoroughly blended, incorporate **3 tbsp. (50 mL) melted butter** and **3 tbsp. (50 mL) wine** *or* **cider vinegar**, mixing well. Then fold in ½ **cup (125 mL) chopped nuts** and **1 cup (250 mL) raisins**.

Line a pie plate with **pastry of your choice**. Pour in the pie filling. Cook 5 minutes in a 450°F. (225°C) oven. Then lower heat to 350°F. (180°C) and cook until the filling is firm, or the blade of a knife comes out clean, about 25 to 45 minutes. Remove from oven and cool. To serve, garnish with whipped cream or a meringue made of the 2 remaining egg whites and **4 tbsp. (60 mL) sugar**.

Desserts and Candies

Apple Jam
Confiture de la Confirmation

Almost a lost recipe, this apple jam. I have yet to taste one more delicious. In our family, it was made in the fall and served on special occasions — but especially on Confirmation Day. I remember my Confirmation; the apple jam was placed in a crystal compote dish and served with superb angel food cake. I often serve it with vanilla ice cream.

Peel **enough apples to make 8 lb. (3.6 kg)** (weigh after peeling), then quarter them. Place in a large kettle **5 cups (1.2 L) sugar** and **2 cups (500 mL) cold water.** Bring to a boil, while stirring, and add the peeled apples.

Cook over medium heat for about 30 minutes, stirring often. Add **1 cup (250 mL) rum** and **2 cinnamon sticks.** Boil another 15 minutes or until it passes the jelly test.

While the apple jam is cooking, prepare another **5 lb. (2.25 kg) apples,** peel, quarter, then cut in even slices and place in an earthenware or glass dish. Add **2 cups (500 mL) sugar,** cover, and cook in a 300 °F. (150 °C) oven until the apples are tender, but not mushy. This should take from 40 to 60 minutes.

When the jam is cooked, add the baked apple slices very carefully, without breaking them (a rubber spatula works very well). Pour into jars. Seal with wax.

Dried Fruit Compote
Compote de fruits secs

I vary the fruits according to my fancy; as a matter of fact, it is the only way I truly enjoy dried fruits.

Place in a jam jar, **dried figs** *or* **prunes** *or* **apricots** *or* **peaches** *or* **apples** or a mixture. Add **1 cinnamon stick** *or* **3–4 whole cloves** *or* **orange** *or* **lemon rind**. Place a tablespoon in the jar and pour **boiling green** *or* **black tea** over the fruits. (My grandmother preferred green tea or Chinese smoked tea.) Place the lid on the jar immediately and let it stand 24 hours before using. It must be kept in a cool place.

I sometimes take **1 lb. (500 g) large dried prunes**, place them in a jar, add ½ **tsp. (2 mL) whole cardamon seeds**, ½ **cup (125 mL) dark rum**, ¼ **cup (60 mL) maple syrup**, enough **boiling hot Chinese tea** to cover. Cover and shake. They will keep 6 to 7 months refrigerated.

Here are a few ways to use this compote:

Mash a few prunes, place a dab on a square of Cheddar or Swiss cheese.

Dice and pour over vanilla custard with 1 tbsp. (15 mL) or so of the juice.

Stuff a cored apple with a prune and 1 tsp. (5 mL) of the juice, then bake the apple. Top the baked apple with sour cream. A superb dessert.

Spread on toast or English muffins instead of jam.

The French Colony Molasses Cream
La crème brûlée de la vieille Colonie

The authentic *crème brûlée du Québec* is made with molasses and kernels from peach stones or almond extract. Of course, the kernels from peach stones must be collected in the summer. They are spread on paper to dry, then stored in clean, dry glass jars, in a cool place.

Place in a cast-iron frying pan **1 cup (250 mL) molasses** and **7–10 peach kernels**, slivered. Cook over medium heat until the molasses caramelizes slightly. You can regulate the cooking of the molasses to make it darker or lighter and strongly or more subtly flavored.

To make a blancmange or cornstarch pudding bring to boil **2 cups (500 mL) milk** and thicken with **3 tbsp. (50 mL) cornstarch** mixed with **3 tbsp. (50 mL) cold water**. If you have not added peach kernels to the molasses, add **1 tsp. (5 mL) pure almond extract** *or* **ratafia extract** to the blancmange.

Pour the caramelized molasses into the hot blancmange. Stir to blend thoroughly. Pour into a lightly oiled mold and refrigerate until set. If desired, garnish with chopped nuts and whipped cream.

Nanny's Custard
La cossetarde de Nounou

My grandmother used to serve this delicious custard poured over a mixture of fruits which were cut in small pieces and lightly sweetened. For special occasions, she sprinkled this with finely chopped nuts or finely diced marshmallows, and always served it well chilled. It is easy to prepare and a good way to use up any fruit. This custard goes well with steamed pudding, sponge cake, *pain de Savoie*, gingerbread, or simply as is, well chilled in small crystal bowls.

Mix together ½ **cup (125 mL) milk** with **3 tbsp. (50 mL) flour** until smooth; add to **1¼ cups (310 mL) scalded milk**, heated in the top of a double boiler, and cook, while stirring, until mixture is creamy.

Beat lightly **2 egg yolks**, add ¼ **cup (60 mL) sugar** and ½ **tsp. (2 mL) salt**, and keep on beating until thoroughly blended.

Pour into the hot milk mixture, while beating. Cook in double boiler over hot water until custard is smooth and has a rich creamy texture. Add ½ **tsp. (2 mL) vanilla**.

Blueberry Dumplings
Grands-pères aux bleuets

I never knew why dessert dumplings were called *grands-pères* in Québec. They still bear the same name.

In a large saucepan place **4 cups (1 L) blueberries, 1 cup (250 mL) white** *or* **brown sugar** *or* **molasses** (I prefer molasses), **1 tsp. (5 mL) lemon juice, 1 cup (250 mL) boiling water**. Stir together, cover, and cook 20 minutes over low heat, or until you have a nice syrup.

To prepare the dumpling dough, sift together in a bowl **2 cups (500 mL) all-purpose flour, ½ tsp. (2 mL) salt, 3 tsp. (15 mL) baking powder**. Cut into this mixture **4–6 tbsp. (60–90 mL) shortening** until it resembles coarse breadcrumbs. Gradually add **1 cup (250 mL) milk** *or* **water**. Stir together just enough to blend.

To cook, drop by teaspoonfuls (5 mL) into the blueberry sauce — not more than 7 to 8 dough balls at a time. As soon as all the dough has been dropped in the sauce, cover and cook over medium heat 20 minutes. Remove dough balls from the sauce with a perforated spoon and set on an attractive dish. Pour the remaining blueberry sauce over the dumplings and serve hot with chilled cream, or ice cream, which will melt in the hot sauce.

French Toast for Good Little Children
Le pain doré des bons petits enfants

Pain doré was served for Sunday supper, and if we had been good children, we were given our share. Grandmother served it to us often, but I wonder if we had always really been good!

Mix together in a soup plate **1 beaten egg, 2 tbsp. (30 mL) milk, ¼ tsp. (1 mL) savory**.

Cut **4 slices bread**, soak in the milk, and brown on both sides in a little **butter** *or* **bacon fat**. Place in a baking dish. Cover each slice with **chicken leftovers**, cut in small pieces.

Make a white sauce with **2 tbsp. (30 mL) butter, 2 tbsp. (30 mL) flour, 1 cup (250 mL) milk, salt** and **pepper, a pinch of nutmeg**. Pour some over each toast. Bake 20 minutes in a 375 °F. (190 °C) oven.

Hot Milk Toast
Rôties au lait chaud

To replace the woodstove flavor, I place slices of brown bread on a baking sheet and toast them in a 400 °F. (200 °C) oven. Then I butter each slice with whipped butter, blended with the desired amount of honey, and pour milk on top.

Try it after skiing, adding a little rum or brandy to the hot milk.

Grand-mère wrote in her little book:

> *It is pleasurable to serve these to my grandchildren when they return from midnight mass after the sleigh ride through the cold, snowy, windy night. It is heartwarming to see how they enjoy it.*
>
> *I toast large slices of homemade bread on the woodstove, butter them with my whipped butter, spread each one generously with honey from our bees, place each slice in a soup plate, and pour rich hot milk on top.*

The "Drowned Blueberries" Pudding
Le pâté des bleuets noyés

My grandfather would always say, "Beaucoup de pâté, peu de bleuets" (a lot of pudding, few blueberries). My grandmother would reply, "There are few left, so they must be used sparingly." Thus came about the name of this pudding. I think it definitely tastes of blueberries and the dough is a beautiful color. I make it with frozen, fresh, or canned blueberries, the latter well drained.

Cream ½ **cup (125 mL) shortening** *or* **butter**; add ½ **cup (125 mL) sugar** and **2 beaten eggs.** Beat to a light creamy texture.

Sift together **2 cups (500 mL) all-purpose flour, 2½ tsp. (12 mL) baking powder, ¼ tsp. (1 mL) salt, ¼ tsp. (1 mL) ground cloves.**

Add the flour to the creamed mixture, alternating with ½ **cup (125 mL) milk.** Spread the dough in an 8 x 8 inch (20 x 20 cm) or 7 x 12 inch (17.5 x 30 cm) buttered dish.

Mix **2 cups (500 mL) blueberries** with **2 tbsp. (30 mL) lemon juice**. Spread evenly over the dough.

Mix together **½ cup (125 mL) flour**, **½ cup (125 mL) sugar**, **½ tsp. (2 mL) cinnamon**, **¼ cup (60 mL) butter**. When the mixture is mealy, spread over the blueberries. Bake 1 hour in a 350°F. (180°C) oven or until golden brown. Serve warm with cream or lemon sauce.

Caramel Bread Pudding
Pouding au pain au caramel

This pudding was the traditional Holy Saturday dessert on my grandmother's table. To make up for the severity of Lent, which ended at noon, a real feast was served at one o'clock.

Heat **5 cups (1¼ L) milk** *or* **half cream, half milk**. Cube **10 slices bread**, preferably dry, and place in a bowl. Add **¾ cup (180 mL) brown sugar** *or* **maple sugar, 3 tbsp. (50 mL) butter**, the hot milk. Let stand 5 minutes.

Beat **4 eggs** until very light. Beat the bread mixture to make it as creamy as possible, then add the beaten eggs.

Grease a 2-quart (2 L) mold or two 9 x 4 inch (22.5 x 10 cm) bread pans.

Caramelize **1 cup (250 mL) sugar** in a frying pan over medium heat (it melts and takes on a golden color). Pour this syrup in the greased mold and tilt the mold so the caramel will stick to the sides.

Pour the bread mixture into the mold. Place the mold in a saucepan in 1 inch (2.5 cm) of water. Bake 1½ hours at 325°F. (160°C) or until the blade of a knife comes out clean.

Cool 2 to 3 hours at room temperature before serving. Pass a knife all around and unmold; the pudding will be surrounded with a lovely golden sauce. Serve with whipped cream, if desired.

Lake St. John Bread Pudding
Pouding au pain du Lac St. Jean

It is easy to understand why my grandmother chose that name. (Has anyone not heard of the famous Lake St. John blueberries?) This pudding was thought to be worthy of the Sunday table.

Melt ¾ **cup (180 L) butter**. Place in a bowl **4 cups (1 L)** ½-**inch (1.25 cm) bread cubes, 1 tsp. (5 mL) cinnamon, ¼ cup (1 mL) sugar**. Pour the melted butter over this mixture and stir with a fork until the bread is well coated with butter.

Mix together **2 cups (500 mL) fresh** *or* **frozen blueberries, 2 tbsp. (30 mL) lemon juice, ½ cup (125 mL) dark brown sugar**.

Make alternative layers of the blueberries and the bread in a pudding dish. Bake in 350 °F. (180 °C) oven 20 to 40 minutes or until golden brown. Serve hot or cold.

The Inverted Cup Pudding
Pâté à la tasse renversée

These puddings were summer favorites, made with fresh fruit from the market or the garden. They were so named because a cup that had lost its handle was placed in the middle of the old brown earthenware dish (a *tourtière*), the fruits were placed all around the cup, and the dough was spread over the fruit, and surrounding the cup. The inverted cup absorbed the excess juice during the cooking, so there was no spilling over. It also prevented the dough from falling into the juice in the middle of the dish. Often a pretty porcelain blackbird, with its mouth opened, replaced the old cup. These birds came from England and can still be found.

When the pudding was ready to be served, a piece of dough was removed and the cup, filled with beautiful bright juice, was lifted out. What an aroma!

Place a cup in the middle of a pudding dish. Place **2–4 cups (500–1000 mL) fruit of your choice** (peaches, pears, strawberries, blueberries, raspberries, apples, or combination of any fruits) all around, sprinkle with ¾–**1 cup (180–250 mL) brown sugar**, and dot with **1 tbsp. (15 mL) butter**.

Sift together 1½ cups (375 mL) all-purpose flour, 2 tsp. (10 mL) baking powder, ¼ tsp. (1 mL) salt, and cut in 2 tbsp. (30 mL) shortening. Mix together 1 well-beaten egg and 6 tbsp. (90 mL) milk, add to flour, and mix like biscuit dough. Spread over the fruits with your hands.

Bake 15 minutes at 425°F. (215°C). Remove from oven and top with the following syrup: boil together for 2 minutes ¼ cup (60 mL) sugar, 2 tbsp. (30 mL) boiling water, ¼ tsp. (1 mL) extract of your choice. Return pudding to the oven for another 15 minutes. Serve hot with chilled cream.

Pudding Sauce
Sauce pour pouding

Both Grand-mère and Mother made all types of desserts with their apple peels, as well as a superb jelly. I especially enjoy this sauce and the jelly.

Weigh ½ lb. (227 g) washed peels and cores. Boil them for about 20 minutes with 2 cups (500 mL) water, 1 cinnamon stick, 2 whole cloves. Drain the mixture, pressing hard.

Melt 1 tbsp. (15 mL) butter with 1 tbsp. (15 mL) flour. Add the thickish apple juice and cook to a nice, smooth creamy texture. Sweeten to taste with maple syrup and leave it to simmer gently for 5 to 6 minutes. Also a very good syrup to pour over pancakes.

Aunt Lumeda's Rhubarb Squares
Les carrés de rhubarbe de ma tante Lumeda

Tante Lumeda was the elegant "old maid" of the family. She lived with her sister, then her brother, and finally settled in Edmonton, Alberta. She had a reputation for great desserts.

Mix in a bowl **1 cup (250 mL) all-purpose flour**, ¾ **cup (80 mL) corn flour, 1 well-packed cup (250 mL) dark brown sugar,** ½ **cup (125 mL) melted butter, 1 tsp. (5 mL) cinnamon.**

Butter an 8 x 8 x 2 inch (20 x 20 x 5 cm) cake pan. Press down half the mixture in the bottom. Cover with **4 cups (1 kg) rhubarb,** cut in ½-inch (1.25 cm) pieces.

Place in a saucepan **1 cup (250 mL) sugar, 2 tbsp. (30 mL) cornstarch, 1 cup (250 mL) water, 1 tsp. (5 mL) vanilla.** Bring to boil while stirring, until the sauce is creamy and transparent. Pour over the rhubarb.

Top with the remaining flour mixture. Bake 1 hour in a 350°F. (180°C) oven. Serve hot, cut in squares, with whipped cream.

New Year's Caramels
Le caramel du Jour de l'An

Grandmother used to put these caramels in small wooden shoes that she had painted in gold and garnished with mistletoe. This was not only attractive, but the caramels were the most delicious I have ever eaten.

Whipping cream is a must in this recipe, which is long to make, but to rush it is to spoil it.

Measure **3 cups (750 mL) rich cream** (at Grandmother's cream was lifted from the pans after standing 3 to 4 days).

Place in a large saucepan 1 cup (250 mL) of the cream, **2 cups (500 mL) sugar, 1 cup (250 mL) maple** *or* **corn syrup,** ¼ **tsp. (1 mL) salt.** Stir over low heat until mixture boils. Cook to 234°F. (112°C) on candy thermometer, or until a soft ball forms in cold water.

While stirring, slowly add another cup (250 mL) of the cream, so as not to stop boiling. Add **2 tbsp. (30 mL) butter.** Keep on cooking as before to 234°F.(112°C). Then add the last cup (250 mL) cream in the same manner and **2 tbsp. (30**

mL) butter. This time cook to 246°F. (115°C) on thermometer, or until a soft ball forms in cold water.

Remove from heat, add **1 tsp. (5 mL) vanilla** *or* **maple extract, ¼ tsp. (1 mL) almond extract.** Stir just enough to blend. Pour into a buttered 8 x 8 x 2 inch (20 x 20 x 5 cm) dish. Cool, cut in squares, and wrap individually in gold paper.

If desired, you may add ⅔ cup (160 mL) chopped nuts at the same time as you add the vanilla. To make chocolate caramels, melt 4 squares of unsweetened chocolate, which you add with the vanilla and nuts.

Real "Sucre à la crème" with Syrup
Véritable sucre à la crème avec sirop

When Monsieur le Curé paid my grandparents a visit at the beginning of each month, Hilaire (my grandfather) gave him some of his best eggs, and Grandmother made her Sunday-best *sucre à la crème*, following this recipe:

> *I place* **2 cups (500 mL) maple syrup** *in a large saucepan with* **2 generous spoonfuls of butter,** *and cook slowly until the syrup boils to a very thick consistency, and bubbles all over. I then add* **1 cup (250 mL) of my richest cream,** *slightly warmed. The mixture then boils very rapidly and the syrup hardens, but I let it cook, stirring often, until it becomes creamy. When a small quantity poured over clean snow turns to soft toffee, I remove the pan from the heat, let it cool, and beat until creamy. It is then poured into my lovely white dish, which I have buttered, and garnished with* **black walnuts.** *I cut it at the table as we eat it. It is so good!*

These days, the snow can be replaced by ice water and the candy cooked to a soft ball stage on the candy thermometer. Walnuts can replace the costly black walnuts. This *sucre* remains soft and melts in the mouth.

Of course, mine is never like Grand-mère's — she had thick maple syrup and cream that contained at least 60 to 70% fat.

White "Sucre à la Crème"
Sucre à la crème blanc

I have never seen this recipe elsewhere. Grand-mère made it with shaved maple sugar — often difficult to find nowadays and quite expensive. Pale brown sugar is an honest substitute. As the sour cream she used was lifted from the bowls of milk and was very rich and heavy, I replace it with ½ cup (125 mL) commercial sour cream and ½ cup (125 mL) heavy cream.

A candy thermometer is almost a must to succeed with this superb non-stirred sugar, and it's worth it.

Place in a saucepan **1 cup (250 mL) sugar, 1 cup (250 mL) pale brown sugar** *or* **maple sugar**, grated, **a pinch of salt, 1 cup (250 mL) sour cream** *or* **½ cup (125 mL) each sour cream and heavy cream.** Bring to boil over low heat without stirring. (This will take some time, but it's the only way to cook it.) When the mixture boils, cook over slightly higher heat to 245°F. (118°C) on the candy thermometer, or to the firm ball stage in cold water. Do not stir throughout the cooking.

Remove from heat, cool, add **a pinch of cinnamon, ½ tsp. (2 mL) vanilla, ½ tsp. (2 mL) maple extract, 1 cup (250 mL) chopped nuts,** and stir until sugary. Pour into a buttered dish. Cool.

Know-How: Tricks of the Trade

Aromatic Salt
Sel aromatique

I dry my herbs in the microwave oven very easily: I place the chosen herb on a white paper towel, the stems side by side. I cover them with another towel and place them in the microwave at high for 1 minute, then turn over the 2 sheets of paper (the bottom one is quite wet), leave them at high for another 1½ minutes, then I throw the dried herbs into a bowl. They will stay vividly colored and fragrant for a whole year.

I was a very young child when I first noticed Grand-mère's "aromatic salt," as she called it. Today this type of salt is even sold commercially, and I would not think of being without a bottle of it near my stove. Basically, my formula is the same as my grandmother's, the only difference being that I use various types of flavorings, such as replacing parsley or celery leaves with savory or tarragon or using half basil, half oregano. For any type of salt, I add 1 tbsp. (15 mL) paprika, then I blend the whole mixture with ½ cup (125 mL) of coarse salt. Since I began using this salt in my cuisine, the flavor of my sauces has improved considerably.

Dry together in a heavy paper bag **1 cup (250 mL) celery leaves** *and* **1 cup (250 mL) parsley.** *Tie the bag in the back of the stove* [or any other convenient place]. *After 1 week, crush the 2 dried herbs and put them through a sieve to crumble them into dust. Add* **½ cup (125 mL) coarse salt, 1 tbsp. (15 mL) freshly ground peppercorns, 1 tsp. (5 mL) savory,** *and crush with a wooden pestle. I keep this salt in small, tightly closed bottles. I sprinkle it over cooked foods and salads using as much as I fancy.*

Apple Peel Vinegar
Vinaigre de pelures de pommes

A surprisingly tasty cider vinegar, perfect on a salad of fresh garden lettuce. To filter the vinegar, set a coffee filter over the coffee pot.

My sister Roxina gave me her recipe for vinegar. It was very good — except for pickling — and it is economical. I now keep all my apple peels.

Fill to ¾ a 4-pint (16–18 cups; 4–5 L) earthenware crock with **apple cores and peels,** *cover with cold water, and add* **1 cup (250 mL) molasses.** *Blend thoroughly. Cover with a cheesecloth, and within 3 to 4 weeks the vinegar will be ready for filtering. I find that the best filter is a piece of old, "country woolen blanket." Bottle, if possible, in dark glass bottles.*

Wine Vinegar
Vinaigre de vin

Vinegar was made from leftover wine, a lost art which should be revived! The favorite at Grandmother's was white vinegar prepared with Sauterne wine.

Brands of wine could be mixed successfully, but all reds were placed in one bottle, whites in another. If there happened to be a mother of vinegar, it was added to the leftover wines. (A mother of vinegar is a greyish substance, thick, wrinkled, and viscous looking, which sometimes appears and spreads in wine vinegar. It may be divided and added to the leftover wines as long as it lasts.) The opening was tied closed with a double layer of cheesecloth, and the bottles were kept in the kitchen cupboard. Four months later, the vinegar would be ready. If there was no "mother," the wines were bottled in the same manner, but left in the cupboard for 5 months.

The Power of a Pinch of Sugar
Une pincée de sucre ici et là

A priceless *petit truc de cuisine*, which I always use. It gives a golden color to meat and produces a caramel brown gravy that is most appetizing; with vegetables, it enhances the color and flavor.

When I cook a roast, I sprinkle the bottom of my roasting pan with 1 tsp. (5 mL) sugar. For chops, I sprinkle ½ tsp. (2 mL) sugar in the bottom of the frying pan before adding the meat. The result in both cases is golden brown gravy and well-browned meat.

When I boil vegetables, I always add ¼ tsp. (1 mL) sugar to the water.

Scented Herb Sugars
Sucres parfumés

If ever you try these, you will never go back to those "little bottles of extract."

To make herb sugar, make alternate layers of **fine white granulated sugar** and fresh leaves of **scented geranium** *or* **lemon verbena** *or* **fresh mint,** *or* **wild rose petals,** and store in tightly closed containers. Grand-mère used these throughout the year on fruits, in delicate custards, and to flavor sponge or pound cake or whipped cream. In those days there were no bottled extracts, but even today, I continue to make these delightful sugars.

Lemon or Orange Extract
Essences de citron, d'orange

I have always made my own lemon and orange extracts, to which I add my homemade vanilla extract — 2 vanilla sticks in 2 cups (500 mL) white rum or white brandy. The longer these pure extracts age, the better they are. Never remove vanilla sticks or citrus fruit rinds; after 4 to 5 months, either brandy or rum can be added to refill the bottle.

First peel **lemons** *or* **oranges** very thinly, removing all the white skin. Place the rind in a bottle, add **2 cups (500 mL) white rum** *or* **brandy** *or* **Dutch gin,** then keep adding lemon or orange peel until the bottle is filled.

One teaspoon (5 mL) will beautifully enhance desserts, cakes, pies, cookies, creams or sauces, and even ice cream.

Savory Fat for Cooking
Gras savoureux pour cuisine

I once though this was my grandmother's creation, until I discovered *gras Normand* in France.

*I keep a small white enamelled pail near the kitchen stove, in which I accumulate cooking fats. When the pail is filled, I cook the fat with 1 **uncooked potato**, cut in 2, 1 **large onion**, unpeeled (the peel gives a nice color to the fat), 2 **cups (500 mL) water**. I boil this mixture 15 to 20 minutes, strain it through a very fine sieve, pour it into an earthenware bowl, and let it stand overnight in the cold pantry. The following day, I carefully remove the hard fat on top of the bowl and throw away the water containing the impurities from the fat.*

It makes delicious pie dough, gingerbread molasses and cookies; ideal for greaseless soups and frying potatoes, in stews, to roast meats.

Fat for Deep Frying
Gras pour friture

In the late 1800s, women used to save all the fat from meats, soups, and so on — a custom we should strive to keep.

When deep frying, add a little fresh fat to the used fat, because when fat is used for the second or third time, it has a tendency to froth. To clarify fat, put it through a piece of linen cloth after each use. (Use only linen or heavy cotton, as only these materials will properly strain fat used to deep fry.)

I store the different types of accumulated fats together, in a container, in the freezer. When I have enough, I melt the fat — no need to defrost — by simply running hot water over the bottom of the container; the block of fat will then fall out with just a little prying. Add 1 cup (250 mL) cold water and melt until any small pieces of fat which do not melt turn a golden brown color. Pour into a bowl, cool, and refrigerate until hard. Then remove the hard fat and throw away the water underneath containing little bits of crisp fat. It will keep for 2 to 3 months refrigerated, well covered. Use in any recipe calling for fat.

Chicken Fat
My grandmother taught me to also keep fat from chickens, turkeys, and ducks (never goose fat, as it is too strong). She strained it into a jar and kept it in a cool place to use in spiced cookies, gingerbread, chicken sauce, boiled rice, vegetable and onion soups. The crisp bits and pieces remaining in the sieve were mashed with a little garlic, savory, salt and pepper, then 1 tbsp. (15 mL) melted fat was added, and the mixture was left to harden in a cool place. This resulted in delicious "cretons," at very little cost.

Maple Butter
Beurre d'érable

Every spring I make 8 to 12 jars of maple butter — less costly than buying it and more delicious! I use it as a dessert.

Grand-mère told me that we knew it was cooked when "our nose was happy," meaning when it smelled good.

Place in a large saucepan **1 cup (250 mL) brown sugar, 3 cups (750 mL) maple syrup, 1 cup (250 mL) light cream, ½ cup (125 mL) corn syrup.** *Boil slowly about 20 to 30 minutes, stirring often. When it looks like thick syrup, add* **4 tbsp. (60 mL) butter.** *Stir until creamy. Pour into an elegant glass jar and close tightly. Keep in the cold cellar* [our refrigerator].

I use my electric mixer instead of stirring, as it is quite a long process. Keep a close eye on it, as at one point it should turn into a soft creamy sugar; if it becomes hard, this means it has been overcooked. In this case, add a few spoonfuls of cream to hard butter, and warm it up. Stir just enough to mix, and bottle. It will keep 5 to 8 months.

Turn your Salted Butter into Sweet Butter
Manière de laver le beurre salé en "tinette"

A *tinette* was the name for the wooden tub used to store the butter. In the 1900s it was customary to buy a 10- or 20-lb. (5–10 kg) *tinette* of butter. Grand-mère made all her butter, which won more than her share of country fair Blue Ribbons. She had a special way of making unsalted butter. Believe me, it works, and costs much less than commercial unsalted butter!

Rinse out a bowl in very hot water, and wash your hands thoroughly, so that the least odor will be passed on to the butter. Then rinse both the bowl and your hands under cold running water, to cool them. Take a good piece of butter and manipulate it in a bowl of icy water until it becomes smooth and waxy. Remove it from the water and quickly flatten it between both hands, then pat it lightly to remove all excess water. Keep in a cold place, well covered.

Whipped Butter
Beurre fouetté

To make whipped butter, I beat it in my mixer, then keep it refrigerated in the same earthenware pot my grandmother used; only the little wooden cover has been replaced. I also use this whipped butter to make flavored butter, by adding garlic, green onions, curry, parsley, lemon rind, tarragon, etc.

At Grand-mère's house, we all loved to eat bread toasted on the woodstove and spread with her whipped butter. Unlike cold butter, it did not tear the bread, nor did it make the toast greasy, as very soft butter tends to do. Furthermore, whipped butter lasted longer.

Grand-mère usually prepared 1 lb. (500 g) at a time. When the butter was at room temperature, she beat it with a wooden paddle until it was almost white and resembled frothy cream. She placed it in an earthenware crock and covered it with a white linen cloth, then a wooden lid, and kept it in the cold pantry.

Whipped Table Cream
Crème de table fouettée

Unbelievable but true — try it when you don't have enough rich cream to whip.

Soak **1 envelope unflavored gelatine** in **2 tbsp. (50 mL) cold water** for 5 minutes, then melt over hot water. Slowly add gelatine to **2 cups (500 mL) ordinary cream** and beat until frothy. Let it stand for 1 hour in a cool place, then beat it again to obtain lovely whipped cream which holds its shape.

Glaze for Fruits or Cake
Glace givrée

Grand-mère's mother-in-law taught her an extraordinary way to glaze fruits or the top of a fruit or pound cake.

Place in saucepan **4½ tsp. (22 mL) powdered gum arabic** (which can still be purchased at the drugstore), **1½ cups (375 mL) water**, **¾ cup (200 mL) sugar**, and let it boil for 5 minutes over medium heat. Brush the top of the warm cake with this hot liquid. Decorate with fruits which stick to this frosting, and after 5 minutes brush liquid once more over the cake and the fruits. The cake will have a lovely frosty glaze.

Leftover Cake Icing
Reste de glacage de gateâu

I always make more cake icing than needed, and I keep the excess in a glass jar in a cool place.

To use it, place the jar in a bowl of hot water until the icing reaches the desired consistency. With hot gingerbread, put a spoonful of cold icing over it; the heat melts it.

I warm the icing in my microwave oven at medium heat, for 40 seconds to 1 minute, depending on the quantity. Wouldn't my grandmother have marveled at that!

Fermented Maple Syrup
Sirop d'érable fermenté

*It may happen, on occasion, that maple syrup left in the metal
gallon container will ferment. I empty it into a large enamelled
casserole and bring to boil. I then remove from heat and
remove the scum very carefully. I pour it into glass jars with a
new rubber band and keep it in a cool dry place.*

*If a recipe calls for maple sugar and I have none, I boil some
syrup over low heat, until it comes to the soft ball stage in cold
water. I let it cool and beat it into sugar, and pour it into a
buttered mold. It will dry into a soft sugar loaf.*

*If, on the other hand, the recipe calls for syrup, and I have no
syrup, I break up my maple sugar, add a little water, and cook
it slowly until it becomes syrupy.*

I have often made use of these valuable hints. The only
thing I do differently is that after the fermented syrup has
been boiled, I pass it through a fine sieve.

Never leave syrup in a metal container once it has been
opened; pour into a glass jar and keep refrigerated.

A Little Know-How
Trois petits conseils

To clean my knives, I use a cork dipped in ground pumice.

*So that the juice of fresh tomatoes will not be lost when they
are sliced, I place them head down and slice from top to
bottom, instead of in round circles.*

*Before cooking buckwheat pancakes, I rub the inside of my
frying pan with a raw potato, cut in half, which prevents
sticking and saves fat.*

Cast-Iron Dutch Oven
Le chaudron de fer

I still use my grandmother's Dutch oven and her cast-iron frying pan. Nothing else will ever be able to replace them.

When new, a cast-iron pan can easily rust and food will stick to the bottom. This is how my grandmother taught me to cure a pan.

Before washing it, throw in a large handful of coarse salt, place the pan in a 325°F. (160°C) oven, and heat it for 30 minutes. Then vigorously rub the coarse salt all over with "an old wool rag." The salt will turn black. Wash the pan in hot water and place in the oven for another 20 minutes.

It should be stored uncovered, to prevent it from retaining humidity. The first 7 or 8 times after using it, dry it very well, and to prevent rust, rub it with a pork rind (a slice of bacon will also do). After this, it is well seasoned and will never rust.

Index